Instant Arabic

How to Express 1,000 Different Ideas With Just 100 Key Words and Phrases

by Fethi Mansouri & Yousef Alreemawi

TUTTLE PUBLISHING
Tokyo • Rutland, Vermont • Singapore

Published in 2007 by Tuttle Publishing, an imprint of Periplus Editions (HK) Ltd., with editorial offices at 364 Innovation Drive, North Clarendon, Vermont 05759 U.S.A and 130 Joo Seng Road, #06-01, Singapore 368357.

Library of Congress Cataloging-in-Publication Data
LCC Card Number: 2007921611
ISBN 13: 978-0-8048-3860-3
ISBN 10: 0-8048-3860-7

Distributed by:

North America,
Latin America & Europe
Tuttle Publishing
364 Innovation Drive
North Clarendon,
VT 05759-9436 U.S.A.
Tel: 1 (802) 773-8930
Fax: 1 (802) 773-6993
info@tuttlepublishing.com
www.tuttlepublishing.com

Asia Pacific
Berkely Books Pte. Ltd.
130 Joo Seng Road, #06-01
Singapore 368357
Tel: (65) 6280 1330
Fax: (65) 6280 6290
Email: inquiries@periplus.com.sg
www.periplus.com

Indonesia
PT Java Books Indonesia
Kawasan Industri Pulogadung
Jl. Rawa Gelam IV No. 9
Jakarta 13930
Tel: (62) 21 4682-1088
Fax: (62) 20 461-0207
cs@javabooks.co.id

Printed in Singapore

11 10 09 08 07 6 5 4 3 2 1

TABLE OF CONTENTS

PREFACE

The Arabic writing system in its current form dates back at least 1800 years. The language acquired a divine status when the Koran was revealed to the Prophet Mohammed in 610 AD. Since then it has become an important language not only to Arabs but also to millions of Muslims living in Africa, Asia and Europe.

Arabic is the native language of well over 250 million people, thus ranking it as one of the most widely spoken world languages, behind only Chinese, English, Spanish and Hindi. There are many national and regional varieties of spoken Arabic, such as Egyptian, Iraqi, Tunisian, Moroccan and Lebanese, but the language presented in this book is based on Modern Standard Arabic, understood by all Arabic speakers and used throughout the Arab world in most written and broadcast material.

The Arabic script is written from right to left. It is based on eighteen different letter forms derived from the script that was historically used to represent the Aramaic language of the ancient Middle East. These letters vary in appearance according to their position within the word (initial, middle or final) and whether they connect to the letters before and after them or not. Eight of the letters may be modified by marks (dots) above or below them in order to represent sounds not occurring in ancient Aramaic, resulting in the current complete Arabic alphabet of 28 letters.

Arabic script has many artistic variations that produce beautiful calligraphy in the same way the Chinese language does. Arabic calligraphy has served as a form of decoration particularly in mosques where images of humans and animals are prohibited.

Arabic letters can be divided into two types: those known as connectors (i.e. other letters can be attached to it), and non-connectors (which cannot be attached to other letters). Also, Arabic letters may change according to where they occur in the word (initial, medial or final).

A word on Spoken Arabic

Arabic is one of the few languages in the world (the other prominent languages being German and Greek) where there is a significant difference between the spoken variety and the written variety. Some linguists refer to these as the high variety for written Arabic and the low variety for spoken dialects. For Arabic the differences are not only between the written and spoken varieties, but also amongst the various regional varieties spoken across the Arab world. For this reason, we have opted in this book to use a simplified standard variety based on Modern Standard Arabic that is very close to all the Arabic dialects spoken across the Middle East and North Africa.

A note on pronunciation

For non-native speakers, some Arabic letters such as glottal fricatives and uvular stops are a little strange and can be challenging to pronounce. Therefore, in this volume every Arabic word or phrase is spelled out the way it should be sounded. We have also included a transliteration in the Roman alphabet based on the conventional transliterating system used by the International Phonetic Association symbols.

PRONUNCIATION GUIDE

Arabic Letter	Transcription	Approximate in English
أ	'	a (as in **and**)
ب	b	b
ت	t	t
ث	th	th (as in **th**ree)
ج	j	j (as in **j**elly)
ح	h	does not exist
خ	kh	doesn't exist (as in Spanish J)
د	d	d
ذ	dh	th (as in **th**ere)
ر	r	r
ز	z	z
س	s	s
ش	sh	sh (as in **sh**ine)
ص	s	doesn't exist (similar to **s**un)
ض	d	doesn't exist (similar to **D**on)
ط	t	doesn't exist (similar to **T**okyo)
ظ	z	doesn't exist
ع	`	doesn't exist
غ	gh	doesn't exist (similar to French R)
ف	f	f
ق	q	doesn't exist
ك	k	k

Arabic Letter	Transcription	Approximate in English
ل	l	l
م	m	m
ن	n	n
ه	h	h
و	w	w (as in **w**as)
ي	y	y (as in **y**ellow)

VOWELS

In standard Arabic, there are three short and three long vowels.

Short Vowels

Short vowels are small signs written above or under the letters indicating the consonants after which they are to be pronounced. In modern written texts most short vowels are not indicated. This means that a thorough knowledge of Arabic vocabulary and grammar is necessary to read "unvocalized" written text. A text in which vowels are marked is called "vocalized" text.

Vowel	Sign	English equivalent
a	َ (fat<u>h</u>ah)	as in "**A**msterdam"
i	ِ (kasrah)	as in "**i**nside"
u	ُ (<u>d</u>ammah)	as in "t**o** go"

Long Vowels

The three long vowels are:

Vowel	Sign	English equivalent
aa	ا	as in "f**a**r"
ii	ي	as in "cl**ea**n"
uu	و	as in "n**oo**n"

PART 1

Lists of Words / Expressions

1 Hello marhaban (*marhaban*) مـرحـبـاً

Peace be upon you.*
as-salaamu `alaykum *(assalaamo `alaykom)*
الـسـلام عـلـيـكـم

(*Response to "peace be upon you"*)*
wa`alaykum as-salaam *(wa`alaykom assalaam)*
وعـلـيـكـم الـسـلام

* *Islamic greetings. See 165-169.*

Good morning.
sabaahul khayr *(sabaahel kheir)* صـبـاح الـخـيـر

(Response to "good morning")
sabaahun nuur *(sabaahenoor)* صـبـاح الـنـور

Good evening.
masaa'ul khayr *(masaa'ol kheir)* مـسـاء الـخـيـر

(*Response to "good evening"*)
masaa'un nuur *(masaa'in noor)* مـسـاء الـنـور

Welcome.
ahlan wa sahlan *(ahlan wa sahlan)* أهلاً وسهلاً

Goodbye.
ma` as-salaamah *(ma`as salaamah)* مع السّلامَة

See you later.
'ilaa al-liqaa' *('ilal leqaa')* إلى اللقاء

Have a good night.
tusbih / tusbihiina *(fem.)* *(tosbeh / tosbeheena)*
تُصبِح
`alaa khayr *(`alaa kheir)* تصبحين على خَير

2 Thanks shukran *(shokran)* شُكراً

Thank you! *(sing. male)*
shukran laka *(shokran laka)* شكراً لكَ

Thank you! *(sing. female)*
shukran laki *(shokran laki)* شكراً لكِ

You are welcome. *(Response to "thank you" or "thanks")*
`afwan *(`af one)* عَفواً

Thank you very much.
shukran jaziilan *(shok run jazeelan)* شُكراً جزيلاً

Thanks for the hospitality.
shukran `alad diyaafah *(shok run `alad deyaafa)*
شُكراً على الضيافة

No, thanks.
laa, shukran *(laa, shokran)* لا ، شُكراً

Don't mention it. *(Literally: "No thanks, this is our duty.")* laa shukra `alaa waajib *(laa shokra `alaa waajeb)*
لا شُكر على واجِب

Don't thank me.
laa tashkurnii *(laa tash kor nee)* لا تشكرني

Thank him for me, please.
ushkurhu `annii *(osh korho `annee)* اشكره عني

3 Sorry 'aasif *(aa sef)* آسف

I am sorry! *(male)*
'anaa 'aasif *(anaa aa sef)* أنا آسف

I am sorry! *(female)*
'anaa 'aasifah *(anaa aa se fah)* أنا آسفة

I am sorry, I apologize.
'anaa 'aasif 'udhran *(anaa aasef odh ran)*
أنا آسِف ، عُذراً

I am very sorry.

'anaa 'aasif jiddan *(anaa 'aasef jeddan)*

أنـا آسِـف جـداً

Sorry for disturbing you.

'aasif lil iz`aaj *(aasef lel ez `aaj)* آسف للإزعاج

4 Please

rajaa'an *(rajaa an)* رجـاءً

law samah̲t *(lao samah̲t)* لـو سـمَـحـت

min fad̲lik *(men fad̲ lek)* مـن فـضـلـك

Come in, please!

tafad̲d̲al bid-duk̲h̲uul *(tafad̲d̲al beddo k̲h̲ool)*

تـفـضـّل بـالـدخـول

Sit down, please!

tafad̲d̲al bil-juluus *(tafad̲d̲al bel joloos)*

تـفـضـّل بـالـجـُلـوس

Here you are! Help yourself! Please take!

tafad̲d̲al *(ta fad̲d̲al)* تـفـضـّل

Just a moment, please.

lah̲z̲ah min fad̲lik *(lah̲ z̲ah men fad̲ lek)*

لـحـظـة مـن فـضـلـك

Bring me water, please.

'ahdirlii maa'an min fadlik *(ahder lee maa an men fad lek)*

أحـضـر لــي مــاءً مـن فـضـلـك

Please continue.

istamirr min fadlik *(esta mer men fad lek)*

اســتـمـر مـن فـضـلـك

Please stop.

tawaqqaf arjuuk *(tawaq qaf arjook)* تــوقــف أرجــوك

The bill, please.

alfaatuurah min fadlik *(al faa too rah men fad lek)*

الـفـاتــورة مـن فـضـلـك

Please wait here.

intazir hunaa law samaht *(enta zer honaa lao samaht)*

انــتـظـر هـنـا لـو سـمـحــت

5 Yes na`am (*na`am*) نعم

Yes, that's right.

na`am haadhaa sahiih *(na`am, haa dhaa sa heeh)*

نعــم هذا صحيح

Yes, I have heard of it.

na`am, sami`tu bidhaalik *(na`am, sa me`to be dhaa lek)*

نعم سمعت بذلك

Yes, I would like some.

na`am, ‘uriidu ba`dan minh *(na`am oreedo ba`dan menh)* نعم، أريد بعضاً منه

Yes, I speak Arabic.

na`am, ‘anaa ‘atakallamul `arabiyyah *(na`am, anaa ata kalla mol `ara beyyah)*
نعم، أنا أتكلم العربية

Yes, please.

na`am min fadlik *(na`am, men fad lek)*
نعم، من فضلك

6 No laa *(laa)* لا

No, I am OK.

laa, ana `alaa maa yuraam *(laa, anaa `alaa maa yo raam)* لا، أنا على ما يرام

No problem.

laa mushkilah *(laa mosh kelah)* لا مشكلة

No, thanks.

laa, shukran *(laa, shokran)* لا، شكراً

7 Negation
Negating an activity in the past
ما maa (*maa*) **or** لم lamm (*lamm*)

I didn't sleep well.

'anaa lamm 'anam jayyidan *(anaa lam anam jayye dan)*
أنا لم أنم جيداً

I didn't eat.

'anaa lamm 'aakul *(anaa lamm aa kol)* أنا لم آكل

I didn't come.

'anaa lamm 'aatii *(anaa lamm aa tee)* أنا لم آتي

Negating an activity in the present
لا laa (*laa*)

I don't go.

'anaa laa 'adh-hab *(anaa laa adh hab)* أنا لا أذهب

I don't sleep late.

'anaa laa 'anaamu muta'akh khiran *('anaa laa anaa mo mo ta akh kheran)* أنا لا أنام متأخراً

I don't want.

'anaa laa 'uriid *(anaa laa oreed)* أنا لا أريد

I don't like.

'anaa laa 'uhibbu *(anaa laa oheb bo)* أنا لا أحب

Negating an activity in the future لن lann (*lann*)

I will not go.

'anaa lann 'adh-hab *(anaa lann adh hab)* أنا لن أذهب

I will not sleep here.

'anaa lann 'anaama hunaa *(anaa lann anaa ma honaa)*
أنا لن أنام هنا

I will not come.

'anaa lann 'aatiya *(anaa lann aa teya)* أنا لن آتي

Negating a situation ليس laysa (*laysa*)

I am not from here.

'anaa lastu min hunaa *(anaa lasto men honaa)*
أنا لست من هنا

This car isn't mine.

haadhihis sayyaarah laysat lii
(haa dhe hes sayyaa rah layy sat lee)
هذه السيارة ليست لي

The hotel isn't good.
alfunduq laysa jayyidan *(al fon doq laysa jayye dan)*
الفندق ليس جيداً

8 **I** 'anaa *(anaa)* أنــا

I am here on holiday.
'anaa hunaa fii' ijaazah *(anaa honaa fee ejaa zah)*
أنــا هــنــا فــي إجــازة

I am here on business.
'anaa hunaa fii `amal *(anaa honaa fee `amal)*
أنــا هــنــا فــي عــمــل

I travel alone.
'anaa 'usaafiru wa<u>h</u>dii *(anaa osaa fero wa<u>h</u> dee)*
أنــا أُســافِــر وحــدي

I am not from here.
'anaa lastu min hunaa *(anaa lasto men honaa)*
أنــا لــســتُ مــِن هُــنــا

I know.
'anaa 'a`rif *(anaa a`ref)* أنــا أعــرف

I don't know.
'anaa laa 'a`rif *(anaa laa a`ref)* أنــا لا أعــرف

I am not sure.

lastu muta'akkidan *(lasto mota akkedan)*

لـســتُ مُـتــأكّـداً

I have had enough, thank you!

laqad iktafayt. <u>sh</u>ukran *(laqad ekta fayt shok ran)*

لـقـد اكـتـفـيـت، شـكـراً

9 My … + ii (… + *ee*)... ـــي +...

This is my bag.

haa<u>dh</u>ihi <u>h</u>aqiibatii *(haa <u>dh</u>ehe <u>h</u>aqee batee)*

هـذه حـقـيـبـَتـي

This is my book.

haa<u>dh</u>aa kitaabii *(haa <u>dh</u>aa ketaa bee)* هـذا كِتـابـي

My address is … .

`unwaanii huwa … . *(`on waa nee howa … .)*

عـنـوانـي هـو ... .

10 You

You *(sing. masc.)* 'anta *(anta)* أنـتَ

You *(sing. fem.)* 'anti *(ante)* أنـتِ

You *(dual)* 'antumaa *(antomaa)* أنـتُـمـا

You *(pl. masc.)* 'antum *(antom)* أنـتُـم

You *(pl. fem.)* 'antunna *(antonna)* أنـتُـنَّ

Where are you from?

min 'ayna 'anta? (men ayna anta?) مِــن أين أنتَ؟

Are you Chinese?

hal 'anta s̲iiniyy? *(hal anta see nee?)*

هـل أنتَ صـيـنـيّ؟

Do you live here?

hal ta`iis̲hu hunaa?*(hal ta `eesho honaa?)*

* هـل تـعـيـشُ هُنا ؟

** Verbs in Arabic conjugate according to the doer/agent,
this means that* تـعـيـش *itself means "you live."*

Are you married?

hal 'anta mutazawwij? *(hal anta mota zawwej?)*

هـل أنـتَ مُـتـزوّج

11 He / She

he: huwa *(ho wa)* هـو
she: hiya *(heya)* أنـتَ صـيـنـيّ؟

Who is he?

man huwa? *(man ho wa?)* مِــن هـو؟

She is my wife.

hiya zawjatii *(heya zawjatee)* هـي زوجـتـي

Is he Jordanian?

hal huwa urduniyy? *(hal ho wa ordonee?)*

هـل هـو أردنــيّ؟

Is she married?

hal hiya mutazawwijah? *(hal heya mota zaw wejah?)*

هـل هـي مـتـزوجـة؟

He took my room keys.

a<u>kh</u>a<u>dh</u>a mafaatii<u>h</u>a <u>gh</u>urfatii

(a<u>kh</u>a<u>dh</u>a mafaa tee<u>h</u> <u>gh</u>or fatee)

أخـذ مـفـاتـيـح غـرفـتـي *

12 We / They

we: na<u>h</u>nu *(na<u>h</u>no)* نـحـن

they: hum *(hom)* هـم

Where are we?

'ayna na<u>h</u>nu? *(ayna na<u>h</u>no?)* أيـن نـحـن؟

Where are they?

'ayna hum? *(ayna hom?)* أين هـم؟

We are Australians.

na<u>h</u>nu 'usturaaliyyuun *(na<u>h</u>no osto raaleyyoon)*

نـحـن أسـتـرالـيـون

They are from Syria.

hum min suuryaa *(hom men sooryaa)*

هـم مـن سـوريـا

We are going to the market.

na<u>h</u>nu <u>dh</u>aahibuun ‘ilas suuq

(na<u>h</u>no <u>dh</u>aa heboona elas sooq)

نـحـن ذاهِـبـون إلـى السـوق

They are from Indonesia.

hum min ‘indunisyaa *(hom men endo nees yaa)*

هـم مـن إنـدونـيـسـيـا

They don’t speak Arabic.

hum laa yatakallamoonal `arabiyyah

(hom laa yata kallamoonal `ara beyyah)

هـم لا يـتـكـلـمـون الـعـربـيـة

or

laa yatakallamoonal `arabiyyah

(laa yata kallamoonal `ara beyyah)

لا يـتـكـلـمـون الـعـربـيـة *

We stay in this hotel.

na<u>h</u>nu naskun fii haa<u>dh</u>al funduq

(na<u>h</u>no nas kono fee haa <u>dh</u>al fon doq)

نـحـن نـسـكـنُ فـي هـذا الـفـنـدق

or

naskun fii haadhal funduq
(nas kono fee haa dhal fon doq)
نـسـكـن فـي هـذا الـفـنـدق *

In verbal sentences, the subject (I, we, they...) is clearly indicated in the structure, so it is not necessary to mention it every time you use a verb. For instance, let's take the verb* ***took* *(akhadha) as an example:*

He took. ‘akhadha *(akha dha)* أخـذ
She took. ‘akhadhat *(akha dhat)* أخـذت
I took. ‘akhadhtu *(akhadh to)* أخـذتُ
We took. ‘akhadhnaa *(akhadh naa)* أخـذنـا
They took. ‘akhadhuu *(akha dhoo)* أخـذوا

13 Name ism *(esm)* اســم

My name is ... .
ismii ... . *(esmee ... .)* . ... اسـمـي

What is your name? *(masc.)*
mas muka? *(mas moka?)* ما اسـمُـكَ؟

What is your name? *(fem.)*
mas muki? *(mas moke?)* ما اسـمـكِ

What is your family name?
mas mu `aa'ilatik? *(mas mo `aa ela tek?)*
ما اسمُ عائلتك؟

My family name is … .
ismu `aa'ilatii … . *(esmo `aa ela tee … .)*
اسم عائلتي … .

What's the name of this place?
masmu haadhal makaan? *(masmo haadhal makaan?)*
ما اسم هذا المكان؟

I like your name.
ismuka yu`jibunii *(esmoka yu` jebonee)*
اسمك يعجبني

How do you spell your name?
kayfa tuhajjis mak? *(kayfa tohajjes mak?)*
كيف تهجي اسمك؟

Is your name Arabic?
halis muka `arabiyy? (hales moka `arabee?)
هل اسمك عربي؟

14 Speak / Say

to speak: yatakallam *(yata kallam)* يتكلّم
to say: yaquul *(ya qool)* يقول

Do you speak English?
hal tatakallamul ‘inghliiziyyah?
(hal tata kallamol engleezeyyah?)
هـل تـتـكلّم الإنـجـلـيزيـة؟

I don’t speak Arabic.
‘anaa laa ‘atakallamul `arabiyyah *(anaa laa ata kallamol `arabeyyah)* أنـا لا أتـكلّـم الـعـربـيـة

I speak a little Arabic.
‘atakallamal `arabiyyata qaliilan *(ata kalla mal `arabeyyata qaleenal)* أتـكلّـم الـعـربـيـة قـلـيـلاً

Speak to me slowly, please.
‘arjuu ‘an tatakallama ma`ii bibut’ *(arjoo an ta ta kalla ma ma`ee be bot’)*
أرجـو أن تـتـكلّـم مـعـي بـبُـطء

What are you saying?
maadhaa taquul? *(maadhaa taqool?)* مـاذا تـقـول؟

Please say it again.
‘arjuu ‘an tu`iida ma qultah *(arjoo an to`eeda maa qoltah)* أرجـو أن تُـعـيـد مـا قُـلـتَـه

What is he saying?
maadhaa yaquul? *(maadhaa yaqool?)* مـاذا يـقـول؟

15 **Understand** yafham *(yaf ham)* يفـــهـم

I understand.
‘anaa afham *(anaa afham)* أنا أفـــهـم

I didn’t understand.
‘anaa lam ‘afham *(anaa lam afham)* أنا لم أفـــهـم

I don’t understand what you are saying.
laa ‘afhamu maa taquul (laa afhamo maa taqool)
لا أفــهـم مــا تـقول

Do you understand me?
hal tafhamunii? *(hal tafhamonee?)* هل تـفـهـمُنــي؟

Did you understand me?
hal fahimtanii? *(hal fahem tanee?)* هل فــهمــتنــي

16 **Write** yaktub *(yak tob)* يـكـتـب

I write.
‘anaa ‘aktub *(anaa aktob)* أنــا أكتب

I didn’t write.
lam ‘aktub *(lam aktob)* لــم أكـتـب

I will write to you.
sa ‘aktubu lak *(sa aktob lak)* ســأكـتـب لـك

Who wrote that?

man kataba <u>dh</u>aalik? *(man kataba <u>dh</u>aa lek?)*

مـن كـتـب ذلـك؟

Write your name here!

uktub ismaka hunaa! *(oktob esmak honaa!)*

اكـتـب اسـمـك هـنـا!

Where shall I write my name?

'ayna 'aktubus mii? *(ayna aktobo es mee?)*

أيـن أكتـب اسـمـي؟

Is my name written?

halis mii maktuub? *(hal es mee mak toob?)*

هـل اسـمـي مـكـتـوب؟

Please write it down.

sajjil <u>dh</u>aalik `indak min fa<u>d</u>lik

(sajjel <u>dh</u>aalek `endak men fa<u>d</u> lek)

سـجـل ذلـك عـنـدك

Please write for me your phone number.

uktub lii raqam haatifik law sama<u>h</u>t *(oktob lee raqma haatefek lao sama<u>h</u>t)*

اكـتـب لـي رقـم هـاتـفـك لـو سـمـحـت

Please write that to me in Roman letters.
'arjuu 'an taktuba <u>dh</u>aalik lii bi 'a<u>h</u>rufin rumaniyyah *(arjoo an taktoba <u>dh</u>aa leka lee be a<u>h</u>rofen romaneyyah)*
أن تـكـتـب ذلـك لـي بـأحـرف رومـانـيـة

17 Read yaqra' *(yaqra')* يقـرأ

I read.
'anaa 'aqra' *(anaa aq ra')* أنـا أقـرأ

I read that in the newspaper.
qara'tu <u>dh</u>aalika fil jariidah *(qara'to <u>dh</u>aa leka fel ja ree dah)* قرأت ذلك في الجريدة

Did you read that?
hal qara'ta <u>dh</u>aalik? *(hal qara'ta <u>dh</u>aa lek?)*
هـل قـرأت ذلـك؟

I would like to read this book.
'awaddu 'an 'aqra'a <u>dh</u>aalikal kitaab *(awaddo an aqra'a <u>dh</u>aa lek)* أود أن أقرأ ذلـك الكـتـاب

I cannot read Arabic.
laa 'asta<u>t</u>ii`u qiraa'atal `arabiyyah *(laa asta tee`o qeraa atal `arabeyyah)*
لا أسـتـطـيـع قـراءة الـعـربـيـة

Please read that for me.
'arjuu 'an taqra' <u>dh</u>aalika lii
(arjoo an taq ra a <u>dh</u>aa leka lee)
أرجـو أن تـقـرأ لـي ذلـك لـي

Can you read English?
hal tastaṯii`u 'an taqra'al 'inkliiziyyah? *(hal tasta ṯee`o an taq ra al engleezeyyah?)*
هـل تـسـتـطـيـع أن تـقـرأ الإنـكـلـيـزيـة؟

18 Walk yam<u>sh</u>ii *(yam <u>sh</u>ee)* يـمـشـي

Let's go for a walk!
falnatama<u>sh</u>-<u>sh</u>aa qaliilan! *(fal nata ma<u>sh</u> <u>sh</u>aa qalee lan)* فـلـنـتـمـشّـى قـلـيـلا

I prefer to walk.
'ufa<u>dd</u>il 'an 'am<u>sh</u>ii *(ofa<u>d</u> <u>d</u>elo an am<u>sh</u>ee)*
أفـضّـل أن أمـشـي

Is it too far to walk to the place?
hal al-makaan ba`iidun ma<u>sh</u>yan? *(hal almakaan ba`eed m<u>as</u>h yan?)* هـل الـمـكـان بـعـيـد مـشـيـاً؟

Can I walk to there from the hotel?
hal yumkinunii 'an 'am<u>sh</u>ii 'ilaa hunaak minal funduq? *(hal yomkenonee an am<u>sh</u>ee elaa honaak menal fondoq?)*
هـل يـمـكـنـنـي أن أمـشـي إلـى هـنـاك مـن الـفـنـدق؟

I can't walk.
laa asta tii`u ‘an ‘amshii *(laa asta tee`o an amshee)*
لا أستطيع أن أمشي

You are walking fast.
‘anta tamshii bisur`ah *(anta tamshee be sor`ah)*
أنت تمشي بسرعة

Walk slower!
imshi bi sur`ah! *(emshe be sor`ah!)* امش بسرعة!

19 **Go** yadh-hab *(yadh hab)* يذهب

I am going.
‘anaa dhaahib *(anaa dhaa heb)* أنا ذاهب

I am not going.
‘anaa lann adh-hab *(anaa lann adh hab)* أنا لن أذهب

Are you going?
hal’ anta dhaahib? *(hal anta dhaa heb?)*
هل أنت ذاهب؟

Is she going?
hal hiya dhaahibah? *(hal heya dhaa hebah?)*
هل هي ذاهبة؟

Let's go shopping!

falna<u>dh</u>-hab lit-tasawwuq! *(fal na<u>dh</u> hab let tasawwoq)* فــلــنــذهــب لــلــتــســوُّق

Are we going now?

hal na<u>h</u>nu <u>dh</u>aahibuunal 'aan? *(hal na<u>h</u>nu <u>dh</u>aa heboon al aan?)* هـل نــحــن ذاهــبــون الآن؟

I have to go.

`alayya 'an 'a<u>dh</u>-hab (`alayya an a<u>dh</u> hab) علــي أن أذهــب

I want to go.

'uriidu 'an 'a<u>dh</u>-hab *(oreedo an a<u>dh</u> hab)* أريــد أن أذهــب

Let's go!

fal na<u>dh</u>-hab! *(fal na<u>dh</u> hab!)* فــلــنــذهــب!

Where are you going?

ilaa 'ayna 'anta <u>dh</u>aahib? *(elaa ayna anta <u>dh</u>aa heb?)* إلــى أيــن أنــت ذاهــب؟

20 Come ya'tii *(ya 'tee)* يــأتــي

I am coming.

'anaa 'aatin / qaadim *(anaa aaten / qaadem)* أنــا آتٍ / قــادم

I will not come.
'anaa lan 'aatii *(anaa lan aa tee)* أنــا لــن آتــي

I cannot come.
laa 'astatii `ul quduum *(laa asta tee `ol qodoom)*
لا أســتــطــيــع الــقــدوم

They are coming.
hum qaadimuun *(hom qaa demoon)* هــم قــادمــون

He is coming.
huwa qaadim *(ho wa qaadem)* هــو قــادم

She is coming.
hiya qaadimah *(heya qaademah)* هــي قــادمــة

We are coming.
nahnu qaadimuun *(nahno qaa demoon)*
نــحــن قــادمــون

I will come tomorrow.
sa'aatii ghadan *(sa aatee ghadan)* ســآتــي غــداً

Is he coming with us?
hal huwa qaadimun ma`anaa?
(hal ho wa qaademon ma`anaa?)
هــل هــو قــادم مــعــنــا؟

Come with me.
ta'aala ma`anaa *(ta `aala ma`a naa)* تـعـال مـعـنـا

Is he coming this afternoon?
hal huwa qaadim? *(hal ho wa qaadem?)*
هـل هـو قـادم؟

I don't think they are coming.
laa 'azunnu 'annahum qaadimuun
(laa azonno annahom qaa demoon)
لا أظن أنـهم قـادمـون

Where are you coming from?
min 'ayna 'atayt? *(men ayna atayt?)* مـن أيـن أتـيـت؟

21 Want yuriid *(yoreed)* يـريـد

I want.
'anaa 'uriid *(anaa oreed)* أنـا أريـد

I don't want.
'anaa laa 'uriid *(anaa laa oreed)* أنـا لا أريـد

Do you want?
hal turiid? *(hal toreed?)* هـل تـريـد؟

Who wants to eat?
man yuriidu ‘an ya’kul? *(man yoreedo an ya’ kol?)*
مـن يـريـد أن يـأكـل؟

I want to go to the Pyramids.
‘uriid ‘an ‘adh-haba’ ilal ‘ahraamaat
(oreedo an adh haba elal ahraa maat)
أريـد أن أذهـب إلـى الأهـرامـات

I want to buy a newspaper.
‘uriidu ‘an ‘ashtarii jariidah *(oreedo an ashtaree jareedah)* أريـد أن أشـتـري جـريـدة

I want to sleep.
‘uriidu ‘an ‘anaam *(oreedo an anaam)* أريـد أن أنـام

Do you want to come with us?
hal turiidu ‘an ta’tii ma`anaa? *(hal toreedo an ta’tee ma`anaa?)* هـل تـريـد أن تـأتـي مـعـنـا؟

22 Need yahtaaj *(yah taaj)* يـحـتـاج

I don’t need it, thanks.
laa ‘ahtaajuh, shukran *(laa ah taajoh, shokran)*
لا أحتـاجـه، شـكـرا

Do you need it?
hal tahtaahuh? *(hal tah taajoh?)* هـل تـحـتـاجـه؟

How much money do you need?
kam minan nuquudi tahtaaj? *(kam menan noqood tah taaj?)* كم من النقود تحتاج؟

I need headache pills.
'ahtaaj' ilaa hubuub sudaa` *(ah taajo elaa hoboob sodaa`)* أحتاج إلى حبوب صداع

I need shaving cream.
'ahtaaju' ilaa ma`juun hilaaqah *(ah taajo elaa ma`joon helaa qah)* أحتاج إلى معجون حلاقة

I need an umbrella.
'ahtaaju' ilaa mizallah *(ah taajo elaa mezallah)* أحتاج إلى مظلة

I need batteries.
'ahtaaju' ilaa battaariyyaat *(ah taajo elaa battaa reyyaat)* أحتاج إلى بطاريات

23 Eat ya'kul *(ya' kol)* يأكل

What do you want to eat?
maadhaa turiidu an ta'kul?
(maa dhaa toreedo an ta' kol?) ماذا تريد أن تأكل؟

What time do you eat?
mataa ta'kul *(mataa ta' kol?)* متى تأكل؟

Let's go out to eat something.

falnadh-hab lina'kula shay'an

(fal nadh hab le na'kol shay an)

فلنذهب لنأكل شيئاً

I would like to eat.

'awaddu 'an 'aakul *(awaddo an aakol)* أود أن آكل

I cannot eat all of this.

laa 'astatii`u 'an 'aakula kulla hadhaa *(laa asta tee`o an aakola kolla haadhaa)* أستطيع أن آكل كل هذا

I want to eat.

'uriidu 'an 'aakul *(oreedo an aakol)* أريد أن آكل

I would like to eat it.

'awaddu 'an 'aakula min dhaalik

(awaddo an aakola men dhaa lek)

أود أن آكل من ذلك

Where do you want to eat?

'ayna turiidu 'an ta'kul? *(ayna toreedo an ta' kol?)*

أين تريد أن تأكل؟

I don't eat it.

laa 'aakuluh *(laa aako loh)* لا آكله

Let's eat!

fal na'kul! *(fal na' kol!)* فلنأكل!

Please eat.

tafaddal kul *(tafaddal kol)* تفضل كل

I haven't eaten since morning.

lam ‘aakul mundhus sabaah
(lam aa kol mondhos sabaah)
لم آكل منذ الصباح

24 Drink yashrab *(yash rab)* يشرب

What do you want to drink?

madhaa turiidu’ an tashrab?
(maa dhaa to reedo an tash rab?)
ماذا تريد أن تشرب ؟

I will drink coffee, please.

sa‘ashrabu qahwah law samaht *(sa ash rabo qah wah lao samaht)* سأشرب قهوة لو سمحت

I want to drink.

‘uriidu ‘an ‘ashrab *(oreedo an ashrab)* أريد أن أشرب

I would like to drink some water, please.
‘awaddu ‘an ‘ashraba ba`dal maa’ min fadlik
(awaddo an ashraba ba`dal maa’ men fad lek)
أود أن أشرب بعض الماء من فضلك

I’d like to drink beer.
‘awaddu ‘an ‘ashraba biirah
(awaddo an ashraba beera) أود أن أشرب بيرة

I don’t drink that.
laa ‘ashrabu dhaalik *(laa ashra bo dhaa lek)*
لا أشرب ذلك

I don’t want to drink.
laa ‘uriidu ‘an ashrab *(laa oreedo an ashrab)*
لا أريد أن أشرب

I drank.
‘anaa sharibt *(anaa sharebt)* أنا شربت

Let’s drink!
fal nashrab! *(fal nash rab!)* فلنشرب!

Please drink.
tafaddal ishrab *(tafaddal ishrab)* تفضل اشرب

Please don't drink.
laa ta<u>sh</u> rab min fa<u>d</u>lik *(laa ta<u>sh</u>rab men fa<u>d</u> lek)*
لا تـشـرب مـن فـضـلـك

Would you like something to drink?
hal tawaddu an ta<u>sh</u>raba <u>sh</u>ayy'an?
(hal tawaddo an ta<u>sh</u>raba <u>sh</u>ayy an)
هـل تود أن تـشـرب شـيـئاً؟

25 Like / Don't like
yu<u>h</u>ibbu / laa yu<u>h</u>ibbu *(yo<u>h</u>ebbo / laa yo<u>h</u>ebbo)*
يحب / لا يحـب

I like.
'u<u>h</u>ibbu *(o<u>h</u>ebbo)* أحـب

I don't like.
laa 'u<u>h</u>ibbu *(laa o<u>h</u>ebbo)* لا أحـب

I like Chinese food.
'<u>u</u>hibbu- <u>t</u>a`aama<u>s</u> <u>s</u>iiniyy *(o<u>h</u>ebbo a<u>tt</u>a `aama a<u>ss</u>ee nee)*
أحب الـطـعـام الـصـيـنـي

I don't like spicy food.
laa u<u>h</u>ibbut- <u>t</u>a`aamal mubahhar
(laa o<u>h</u>ebbo a<u>tt</u>a `aamal mobahhar)
لا أحب الـطـعـام الـمـبـهـر

I like action movies.

‘uhibbu ‘aflaamal ‘ithaarah *(ohebbo aflaamal ethaa rah)*

أحـب أفـلام الإثـارة

I don't like horror movies.

laa ‘uhibbu ‘aflaamar ru`b *(laa ohebbo aflaamar ro`b)*

لا أحـب أفلام الـرعـب

I like country music.

‘uhibbu musiiqar riif *(ohebbo moseeqar reef)*

أحـب مـوسـيـقـى الـريـف

I don't like rock music.

laa ‘uhibbu musiiqar ruk *(laa ohebbo moseeqar rok)*

لا أحـب مـوسـيـقى الـروك

26 I can / I can't

‘astatii` *(asta tee`)* أستطيع

laa ‘astatii` *(laa asta tee`)* لا أستطيع

I can speak Arabic a little.

‘astatii`u ‘an ‘atakallamal `arabiyyata qaliilan

(asta tee`o an ata kalla mal `arabeyyata qaleelan)

أستطيع أن أتكَلَّم العربية قليلا

I can't speak French.

laa 'astaṭii`u 'an 'atakallamal faransiyyah

(laa asta ṭee`o an ata kalla mal faranseyyah)

لا أستطيع أن أتكَـلَّـم الـفـرنسيـة

I can do that.

'astaṭii`u 'an 'af`ala dhaalik

(asta ṭee`o an af`ala dhaa lek)

أستطيع أن أفعـل ذلك

I can't do that.

laa 'astaṭii`u 'an 'af`ala dhaalik *(laa asta tee`o an*

af`ala dhaa lek) لا أستطيع أن أفعـل ذلك

I can carry that bag.

'astaṭii`u ḥamla tilkal ḥaqiibah *(asta ṭee`o ḥamla tel-*

kal ḥaqeebah) أستطع حمـل تـلك الـحـقـيـبـة

I can't swim.

laa 'astaṭii`u 'an 'asbaḥ *(laa asta tee`o an asbaḥ)*

لا أستطيع أن أسبـح

27 **Have** `indii *(`endee)* عـنـدي

Do you have a car?

hal `indaka sayyaarah? *(hal `endaka sayyaarah?)*

هـل عـنـدك سيـارة؟

I had a car.
kaana `indii sayyaarah *(kaana `endee sayyaarah)*
كان عندي سيارة

Do they have?
hal `indahom? *(hal `endahom?)* هل عندهم؟

Do you have the tickets?
hal `indakat ta<u>dh</u>aakir? *(hal `indakat ta <u>dh</u>aaker?)*
هل عندك التذاكر؟

28 I don't have laysa `indii *(laysa `endee)*
ليس عندي

I don't have my passport.
jawaazu safarii laysa `indii
(jawaazo safa ree laysa `endee)
جواز سفري ليس عندي

I don't have any money.
laysa `indii 'ayyu maal *(laysa `endee ayyo maal)*
ليس عندي أيُّ مال

I don't have an umbrella.
laysa `indii mi<u>z</u>allah *(laysa `endee me<u>z</u>allah)*
ليس عندي مظلّة

I don't have a pen.

laysa `indii qalam (laysa `endee qalam)

لـيـس عـنـدي قـلـم

29 Wait yantaẕir *(yan taẕer)* ينتظر

I wait.

'anaa antaẕir *(anaa anta ẕer)* أنـا أنـتـظـر

Wait for me, please!

intaẕirnii min faḏlik *(enta ẕernee men faḏ lek)*

انـتـظـرنـي مـن فـضـلـك

Let's wait for him!

falnantaẕirh! *(fal nanta ẕerh!)* فـلـنـنـتـظـره!

I was waiting for you.

kuntu 'antaẕiruk *(konto anta ẕerok)* كـنـت أنـتـظـرك

Will you wait?

hal satantaẕir? *(hal sa tanta ẕer?)* هـل سـتـنـتـظـر؟

I waited for too long.

Intaẕartu ṯawiilan *(enta ẕarto ṯaweelan)*

انـتـظـرت طـويـلا

Should we wait?
hal yanbaghii lanal intizaar?
(hal yanbaghee lanal ente zaar?)
هل ينبغي لنا الإنتظار؟

Wait here!
intazir hunaa! *(enta zer honaa)* انتظر هنا!

I will wait for you at the hotel.
sa'antaziruka fil funduq *(sa anta zeroka fel fondoq)*
سأنتظرك في الفندق

Don't wait!
mamnuu` alintizaar! *(mamnoo` alentezaar!)*
ممنوع الانتظار!

Waiting list
qaa'imat intizaar *(qaa emat entezaar)*
قائمة انتظار

30 Do yaf`al يفعل

I do. 'anaa af`al *(anaa af `al)* أنا أفعل

I will do that.
'anaa sa'af`al dhaalik *(anaa sa af`al dhaa lek)*
أنا سأفعل ذلك

I have to do it.

`alayya 'an 'af`ala <u>dh</u>aalik

(`alayya an af `ala <u>dh</u>aalek) علـي أن أفعلـه

You should do that.

`alayka 'an taf`ala <u>dh</u>aalik

(`alayka an taf`ala <u>dh</u>aalek) عليـك أن تـفـعـل ذلك

I am not going to do that.

lann af`ala <u>dh</u>aalik *(lan af`ala <u>dh</u>aa lek)*

لـن أفـعـل ذلـك

What would you do?

maa<u>dh</u>aa sataf`al? *(maa<u>dh</u>aa sataf `al?)*

مـاذا سـتـفـعـل؟

I did it.

'anaa fa`altuhaa *(anaa fa`altohaa)* أنـا فعـلـتـها

What shall I do?

maa<u>dh</u>aa `alayya 'an 'af`al?

(maa<u>dh</u>aa `alayya an af `al?) مـاذا عـلـيّ أن أفـعـل؟

What do you want to do?

maa<u>dh</u>aa turiidu 'an taf`al?

(maa<u>dh</u>aa toreedo an taf `al) مـاذا تـريـد أن تـفـعـل؟

What is he doing?
maadhaa yaf`al? *(maadhaa yaf`al?)* مـــاذا يــفــعــل؟

31 Who? / Whom? / Whose?
mann *(mann)* مـــن

Who are you?
mann ‘anta? *(mann anta?)* مَــن أنـــت؟

Who is that man?
mann dhaalikar rajul? *(mann dhaa lekar rajol?)*
مَــن ذلـــك الـــرجُـــل؟

Who speaks English here?
mann yatahaddathul inghliiziyyata hunaa?
(mann yata haddathol engleezeyyata honaa?)
مـــن يـــتـــحـــدّث الإنـــجـــلـــيـــزيـــة هـــنـــا؟

Whose car is this?
sayyaratu mann haadhih? *(sayyarato mann haa dheh?)*
ســـيـــارة من هـــذه؟

Whose bags are those?
haqaa’ibu mann tilk? *(haqaa ebo mann telk?)*
حقائب من تلك؟

Whom are you talking to?

ma`a mann tatakallam? *(ma`a mann ta takal lam?)*

مـع مـن تـتـكـلـم؟

32 What?

maa<u>dh</u>aa? *(maa <u>dh</u>aa?)* مـاذا؟

maa *(maa)* مـا؟

What are you saying?

maa<u>dh</u>aa taquul? *(maa <u>dh</u>aa taqool?)* مـاذا تـقـول؟

What is this?

maa ha<u>dh</u>aa? *(maa haa <u>dh</u>aa?)* مـا هـذا؟

What does this mean in Arabic?

maa ma`naa <u>dh</u>aalik bil-`arabiyyah?

(maa ma`naa <u>dh</u>aa lek bel `arabeyyah?)

مـا مـعـنـى ذلـك بـالـعـربـيـة؟

What is your address?

maa `unwaanuk? *(maa `on waanok?)* مـا عـنـوانـك؟

What is the name of this place?

maa ism haa<u>dh</u>al makan? *(mas mo haa dhal makaan?)*

مـا اسـمُ هـذا الـمَـكـان؟

What's wrong?

mal mu<u>sh</u>kilah? *(mal mo<u>sh</u> kelah?)* مـا الـمـشـكـلـه؟

What would you like to eat?
maa<u>dh</u>aa turiidu ‘an ta’kul?
(maa <u>dh</u>aa toreedo an ta’ kol?)
مـاذا تـريـد أن تـأكـل؟

What would you like to drink?
maa<u>dh</u>aa turiido ‘an ta<u>sh</u>rab?
(maa <u>dh</u>aa toreedo an ta<u>sh</u> rab?)
مـاذا تـريـد أن تـشـرب؟

33 When? / What time?
mataa? *(mataa?)* مـتـى؟

When will we go?
mataa sana<u>dh</u>hab? *(mataa sa na<u>dh</u> hab?)*
متى سـنـذهـب؟

When does the market open?
mataa yafta<u>h</u>us suuq? *(mataa taf ta<u>h</u> assooq?)*
مـتـى يـفـتـح الـسـوق؟

When do you have to go?
mataa yajibu ‘an ta<u>dh</u>-hab? *(mataa yajebo an ta<u>dh</u> hab?)* مـتـى يـجـب أن تـذهـب؟

What time is it?
kamis saa`ah? *(kames saa `ah?)* كـم الـسـاعـة؟

What time are we leaving?
mataa sanughaadir? *(mataa sanoghaa der?)*
متى سنغادر؟

What time does the bus leave?
mataa yughaadirul baas? *(mataa sayo ghaaderol baas?)*
متى يغادر الباص؟

What time is breakfast?
matal 'iftaar? *(matal ef taar?)* متى الإفطار؟

What time is lunch?
matal ghadaa'? *(matal ghadaa?)* متى الغداء؟

What time is dinner?
matal `ashaa'? *(matal `ashaa?)* متى العشاء؟

What time does the museum open?
mataa yaftahul muthaf? *(mataa yaftahol mot haf?)*
متى يفتح المتحف؟

What time does the film start?
mataa yabda'ul film? *(mataa yab da ol felm?)*
متى يبدأ الفيلم ؟

34 **Where?** ayna *(ayna)* أيــن

Where is the restaurant?
aynal mat`am? *(aynal mat `am?)* أيــن المَـطــعَـم؟

Where is the hotel?
aynal funduq? *(aynal fon doq?)* أيــن الـفـُـنــدُق؟

Where are you from?
min ‘ayna ‘anta? *(men ayna anta?)* مِن أيــن أنــت؟

Where are we going?
‘ilaa ‘ayna nahnu dhaahibuun?
(elaa ayna nahno dhaa heboon?)
إلى أين نـحـنُ ذاهــبــون؟

Where do you want to go?
‘ilaa ‘ayna turiidu ‘an tadh-hab?
(elaa ayna toreedo an tadh hab?)
إلــى أيــن تــريد أن تــذهــب؟

Where is the bus stop?
‘ayna mawqiful baas? *(ayna mao qefol baas?)*
أيــن مــوقــف الــبــاص؟

Where is the toilet?
‘aynal hammaam? *(aynal hammaam?)* أيــن الــحــمّــام؟

35 How many? / How much? / How long? kam? *(kam?)* كـم؟

How much does this shirt cost?

bi kam haa<u>dh</u>al qamii<u>s</u>? *(bekam haa <u>dh</u>al qa mee<u>s</u>?)*

بـكـم هـذا الـقـمـيـص؟

How long will you stay here?

kam satabqaa hunaa? *(kam satab qaa honaa?)*

كـم سـتـبـقـى هنا؟

How long does the train trip to Alexandria take?

kam muddatur ri<u>h</u>latu bil-qi<u>t</u>aar 'ilal 'iskandariyyah? *(kam modda tor re<u>h</u>lato bel qe<u>t</u>aar elal eskan dareyyah?)*

كـم مُـدَّة الـرحـلـة بـالـقـطـار إلـى الإسـكـنـدريـة؟

How many people would be there?

kam minan nasi sayakuunu hunaak? *(kam menan naase saya koono honaak?)*

كـم مـن الـنـاس سـيـكـون هـنـاك؟

36 How? kayfa? *(kayy fa?)* كـيـف؟

How are you?

kayfa <u>h</u>aaluk? *(kayy fa <u>h</u>aaloka?)* كـيـف حـالـك؟

How can I go to the market?

kayfa yumkin an adh-haba ‘ilas suuq?

(kayfa yomkeno an adh haba elas sooq?)

كـيـف يـمـكـن أن أذهـب إلـى الـسـوق؟

How can I help you?

kayfa yumkinunii musaa`adatuk?

(kayfa yom keno nee mosaa `adatok?)

كيف يمكنني مساعدتك؟

How did you arrive here?

kayfa wasalta ‘ilaa hunaa? *(kayfa wasal ta elaa honaa?)*

كـيـف وصـلـت إلـى هـنـا؟

37 This

this *(masc.)* haadhaa *(haa dhaa)* هـذا

this *(fem.)* haadhihi *(haa dhehe)* هـذه

This is mine.

haadhaa lii *(haa dhaa lee)* هـذا لـي

What is this?

maa haadhaa? *(maa haa dhaa?)* مـا هـذا؟

How much is this pen?

bikam haadhal qalam? *(bekam haa dhal qalam?)*

بـكـم هـذا الـقـلـم؟

I want to buy these books.

'uriidu 'an 'a<u>sh</u>tarii haa<u>dh</u>ihil kutub *

(*oreedo an a<u>sh</u>ta ree haa <u>dh</u>e hel kotob*)

أريد أن أشتـري هـذه الـكـتـب

* Non-living entities (bags, books, cars, etc) are treated as
  singular feminine objects and are referred to with هذه
  haa<u>dh</u>ihi (haa <u>dh</u>ehe).

I like this.

haa<u>dh</u>aa yu`jibunii (*haa <u>dh</u>aa yu` jebonee*)

هـذا يـعـجـبـنـي

I don't like this.

haa<u>dh</u>aa laa yu`jibunii (*haa <u>dh</u>aa laa yu` jebonee*)

هـذا لا يـعـجـبـنـي

This is a beautiful place.

haa<u>dh</u>aa makaanun jamiil

(*haa <u>dh</u>aa makaanon jameel*) هـذا مكـان جـمـيـل

This is my room.

haa<u>dh</u>ihi <u>gh</u>urfatii (*haa <u>dh</u>ehe <u>gh</u>or fatee*)

هـذه غـرفتـي

This is too expensive.

haa<u>dh</u>aa <u>gh</u>aalin jiddan (*haa<u>dh</u>aa <u>gh</u>aalen jed dan*)

هـذا غـالٍ جـداً

38 That

that *(masc.)* dhaalika *(dhaa leka)* ذلـك
that *(fem.)* tilka *(telka)* تـلك

These* are my bags.
tilka haqaa'ibii *(telka ha qaa ebee)* تـلـك حـقـائـبـي

* *Non-living entities (bags, books, cars, etc) are treated as singular feminine objects and are referred to with* تـلك *tilka (telka).*

That is my wife.
tilka zawjatii *(telka zaw jatee)* تـلـك زوجـتي

That is our house.
dhaalika baytunaa *(dhaa leka bayy tonaa)*
ذلـك بـيـتـنـا

How much is that ring?
bikam dhaalikal khaatim?
(bekam dhaa lekal khaa tem?) بـكم ذلـك الـخـاتـم؟

Who is that man?
man dhaalikar rajul? *(man dhaa lekar rajol?)*
مـن ذلـك الـرجل؟

What is the name of that place?

masmu dhaalikal mahal? *(masmo dhaa lekal mahall?)*

ما اسم ذلك المحل؟

39 Here hunaa *(honaa)* هنا

I live here.

'anaa 'askunu hunaa *(anaa askono honaa)*

أسكن هنا

We are not from here.

nahnu lasnaa min hunaa *(nahno lasnaa men honaa)*

نحن لسنا من هنا

Put it here, please.

da`hu hunaa law samaht *(da`ho honaa lao samaht)*

ضعه هنا لو سمحت

I would like to stay here for two more days.

'awaddu 'an 'abqaa hunaa liyawmayn 'idaafiyyayn *(awaddo an abqaa honaa le yawmayn edaa feyyayn)*

أود أن أبقى هنا ليومين إضافيين

The weather here is lovely.

al-jawwu hunaa jamiil *(aljawwo honaa jameel)*

الجو هنا جميل

Who lives here?

man yaskunu hunaa? *(man yaskono honaa?)*
مــن يــســكــن هــنــا؟

I will sit here.

sa'ajlisu hunaa *(sa ajleso honaa)* ســأجــلــس هــنــا

40 **There** hunaak *(honaak)* هــنــاك

Who's there?

man hunaak? *(man honaak?)* مــن هــنــاك؟

I am from Australia. I was born there.

'anaa min 'usturaalyaa, wulidtu hunaak
(anaa men ostoraalyaa, woledto honaak)
أنــا مــن أســتــرالــيــا، وُلــدت هــنــاك

We live there.

nahnu naskunu hunaak *(nahno naskono honaak)*
نــحــن نــســكــن هــنــاك

Are you there?

hal anta mawjuud? *(hal atna mao jood?)*
هــل أنــت مــوجــود؟

Will you be there?

hal satakuunu hunaak? *(hal sata koono honaak?)*
هــل ســتــكــون هــنــاك؟

41 Address `unwaan *(`on waan)* عـنـوان

My address is … .
`unwaanii huwa … . *(`on waanee howa … .)*
عـنـوانـي هـو … .

What is your address?
maa `unwaanuk? *(maa `on waanok?)* مـا عـنـوانـك؟

Please write down your address for me.
'arjuu 'an taktuba lii `unwaanak
(arjoo an tak toba lee `on waa naka)
أرجـو أن تـكـتـب لـي عـنـوانـك لـي

This is my new address.
haadhaa `unwaanil jadiid
(haa dhaa `on waanel ja deed)
هـذا عـنـوانـي الـجديـد

I have changed my address.
laqad ghayyartu `unwaanii
(laqad ghay yarto `on waa nee) لقد غيرت عنواني

Did you change your address?
hal ghayyarta `on waanak?
(hal ghay yarta `on waa nak?) هل غيرت عنوانك؟

42 Introduction ta`aaruf *(ta `aa rof)* تـعـارُف

Allow me to introduce myself.
ismah lii ‘an ‘uqaddima nafsii ‘ilayk
(esmah lee an oqaddema nafsee elayk)
اسمح لي أن أقدم نفسي إليك

Please introduce yourself.
qaddim nafsaka lanaa min fadlik
(qaddem naf saka lanaa men fad lek)
قدم نفسك لنا من فضلك

Please introduce me to her.
‘aujuu ‘an tu’arrifanii `alayhaa *(arjoo an to ’arre fanee `alay haa)* أرجو أن تعرفني عليها

43 Family `aa’ilah *(`aa elah)* عـائـلـة

This is my family.
haadhihi `aa’ilatii *(haa dhehe `aa ela tee)* هذه عائلتي

I live with my family.
‘askunu ma`a `aa’ilatii *(askono ma`a `aa ela tee)*
أسكن مع عائلتي

What is your family name?
masmu `aa’ilatik? *(masmo `aa ela tek?)* ما اسم عائلتك؟

Do you have a family here?
hal `indaka `aa'ilaton honaa?
(hal `endaka `aa elaton honaa?) هل عندك عائلة هنا؟

I need a family car.
'ahtaaju 'ilaa sayyaaratin `aa'iliyyah
(ah taajo elaa sayyaa raten `aa eleyyah)
أحتاج إلى سيارة عائلية

44 Age `umr *(`omr)* عُمر

How old are you?
kam `umruk? *(kam `om rok?)* كم عمرك؟

How old is your husband?
kam `umru zawjuki? *(kam `omro zao jo ke?)*
كم عمر زوجُك؟

Please write your name, age, sex, nationality and address here.
rajaa'an uktub ismaka wa `umrak wa jensaka wa jinsiyyataka wa `un waanak hunaa *(ra jaa an oktob esmaka wa `om raka wa jensaka wa jen seyyataka wa `on waanaka honaa)*
رجاء اكتب اسمك وعمرك و جنسك وجنسيتك وعنوانك هنا

(I am) 40 years old.
`umrii arba`uuna sanah *(`omree arb a `oona sanah)*
عـمـري أربـعـون سـنـة

45 Time al-waqt *(al-waqt)* الوقت

dawn fajr *(fajr)* فـجـر

morning sabaah *(sabaah)* صـبـاح

daytime nahaar *(nahaar)* نـهـار

noon zuhr *(zohr)* ظـهـر

afternoon `asr *(`asr)* بـعـد الـظـهـر

dusk maghrib *(magh reb)* مـغـرب

night layyl *(layyl)* لـيـل

evening masaa' *(masaa')* مـسـاء

hour saa`ah *(saa`ah)* سـاعـة

minute
daqiiqah *(da qee qah)* دقـيـقـة

second
<u>th</u>aaniyah (*<u>th</u>aa neyah*) ثـانـيـة

midnight
munta<u>s</u>af layl (*mon ta<u>s</u>af allayyl*) مـنـتـصـف لـيـل

a.m. <u>s</u>abaa<u>h</u>an (*<u>s</u>abaa<u>h</u>an*) صـبـاحـاً

p.m. masaa'an (*masaa'an*) مـسـاءً

early mubakkir (*mo bakker*) مـبـكّـر

late muta'a<u>kh</u>-<u>kh</u>ir (*mota a<u>kh</u> <u>kh</u>er*) مـتـأخّـر

appointment maw`id (*mao `ed*) مـوعـد

before qabla (*qabla*) قـبـل

after ba`da (*ba`da*) بـعـد

during 'a<u>th</u>naa' (*a<u>th</u>naa'*) أثـنـاء

What time is it?
kamis saa`ah? (*kames saa `ah?*) كـم الـسـاعـة؟

It is one o'clock now.
assaa`atu al-'aan al-waa<u>h</u>idah (*assaa `atol aan al waa <u>h</u>edah*) الـسـاعـة الآن الـواحـدة

2 o'clock ath-thaaniyah *(ath thaaneyah)* الـثـانـيـة

3 o'clock ath-thaalithah *(ath thaalethah)* الـثـالـثـة

4 o'clock ar-raabi`ah *(ar raabe `ah)* الـرابـعـة

5 o'clock al-khaamisah *(al khaamesah)* الخـامـسـة

6 o'clock as-saadisah *(assaa desah)* الـسـادسـة

7 o'clock as-saabi`ah *(assaa be`ah)* الـسـابـعـة

8 o'clock ath-thaaminah *(ath thaa menah)* الـثـامـنـة

9 o'clock at-taasi`ah *(attaa se`ah)* الـتـاسـعة

10 o'clock al-`aashirah *(al`aa sherah)* الـعـاشـرة

11 o'clock
al-haadiyata `ashrata *(alhaa deyata `ash rata)*
الـحـاديـة عـشـرة

12 o'clock
ath-thaaniyata `ashrata *(ath thaaneyata `ashrata)*
الـثـانـيـة عـشـرة

Five past one.
al-waahidah wa khams daqaa'iq
(alwaa hedata wa khams da qaa eq)
الواحدة وخمس دقائق

Ten past two.
ath-thaaniyah wa `ashr daqaa'iq *(ath thaaneyah wa `ashro da qaa eq)* الثانية وعشر دقائق

Quarter past five.
al-khaamisah war-rub` *(alkhaa mesata war rob`)*
الخامسة والربع

Twenty past two.
ath-thaaniyah wath-thuluth
(ath thaaneyah wath tholth) الثانية والثلث

Half past seven.
as-saabi`ah wa nisf *(assaa be`ata wan nesf)*
السابعة والنصف

Quarter to nine.
at-taasi`ah illa rub` *(attaa se`ata ellaa rob`)*
لتاسعة إلا ربع

Twenty to ten.
al-`aashirah illa thulth *(al`aa sherata ellaa tholth)*
العاشرة إلا ثلث

Ten to eleven.
al-haadiyata `ashrata illaa `ashr daqaa'iq
(al haadeyata `ashrata ellaa `ashr da qaa eq)
الحادية عشرة إلا عشرة دقائق

46 Days al'ayyaam *(al'ayyaam)* الأيام

today al-yawm *(al yaom)* اليوم

tomorrow ghadan *(ghadan)* غداً

yesterday 'ams *('ams)* أمس

day after tomorrow ba`da ghad *(ba`da ghad)*
بعد غد

every day kulla yawm *(kolla yaom)* كلّ يوم

day after day
yawm ba`da yawm *(yaom ba`da yaom)*
يوم بعد يوم

tomorrow morning
ghadan sabaahan *(ghadan sabaahan)* غداً صباحاً

Saturday as-sabt *(as-sabt)* السبت

Sunday al-'ahad *(al-'ahad)* الأحد

Monday al-ithnayn *(al eth nayyn)* الإثنين

Tuesday ath-thulaathaa' *(ath tholaa thaa')* الثلاثاء

Wednesday al-'arbi`aa' *(al arbe `aa')* الأربعاء

Thursday al-khamiis *(al khamees)* الخميس

Friday al-jum`ah *(al jom`ah)* الجمعة

I will see you tomorrow.
'araaka ghadan *(araaka ghadan)* أراك غداً

I have a meeting today.
`indii ijtimaa` alyawm *(`endee ejtemaa` al yaom)*
عندي اجتماع اليوم

We arrived yesterday.
wasalnaa 'ams *(wasal naa ams)* وصلنا أمس

We arrived on Wednesday.
wasalnaa yawmal 'arbi`aa'
(wasal naa yaomal arbe `aa') وصلنا يوم الأربعاء

I am leaving on Thursday.
sa'ughaadiru yawmal khamiis
(sa oghaadero yaomal khamees) سأغادر يوم الخميس

47 Weeks
al-asaabii` *(al asaa bee`)* الأسـابـيـع

this week
haadhaa al-usbuu` *(haa dhal os boo`)* هـذا الأسـبـوع

next week
al-usbuu` al-qaadim *(al osboo` al qaadem)*
الأسـبـوع الـقـادِم

last week
al-usbuu` al-maadii *(al osboo` al maadee)*
الأسـبـوع الـمـاضـي

weekend
`utlat nihaayat al-usbuu` *(`otlat nehaaya tel osboo`)*
عـطـلـة نـهـايـة الأسـبـوع

48 Months ash-shuhuur *(ash sho hoor)* الشـهـور

month shahr *(shahr)* شـهـر

next month
ash-shahr al-qaadim *(ash shahr alqaa dem)*
الشــهــر الــقـادم

this month haadhaa ash-shahr *(haa dhash shahr)*
هذا الشــهــر

last month
ash-shahr al-maadii *(ash shahr almaa dee)*
الشهر الماضي

January
yanaayir; kaanuun thaanii *(yanaa yer; kaanoon thaanee)*
يناير / كـانــون ثـانـــي

February
fibraayir; shubaat *(febraayer; sho baat)*
فــبــرايــر / شــبــاط

March
maaris; ‘aa dhaar *(maares; aa dhaar)* مــارس / آذار

April
abriil; niisaan *(abreel; nee saan)* أبريل / نـيـســان

May
maayu; ‘ayyaar *(maa yo; ayyaar)* مــايو / أيــار

June

yuunyu; huzayyraan *(yoonyo; hozayy raan)*
يونيو / حزيران

July

yuulyu; tammuuz *(yoolyo; tammooz)* يوليو / تموز

August

ughustus; ‘aab *(oghos tos; aab)* أغسطس / آب

September

sibtimbar; ‘ayluul *(semtambar; aylool)*
سبتمبر / أيلول

October

uktubar; tishriin awwal *(oktobar; tesh reen awwal)*
أكتوبر / تشرين أول

November

nufambar; tishriin thaanii
(nofambar; tesh reen thaa nee) نوفمبر / تشرين ثاني

December

diisimbar; kaanuun awwal
(dee sembar; kaanoon awwal) ديسمبر / كانون أول

* *Some Arab or Islamic countries also use the Hijrii (emigration) calendar (see pages 74-76) in remembrance*

of Prophet Muhammad's migration from Mecca to Medina. The first day in this calendar was in the lunar month of Muharram, which corresponded to July 16, 622 CE. This date represents a turning point in the history of Islam's beginning and rise and so marks the start of Muslim era or calendar.

The months according to the Hijrii calendar are listed below:

first month muharram *(mo harram)* مُحـرَّم

second month
safar *(safar)* صـفـر

third month
rabii` al-awwal *(ra bee` al awwal)* ربـيـع الأوّل

fourth month
rabii` ath-thaanii *(ra bee` ath thaanee)* ربـيـع الثـاني

fifth month
jumaadaa al-'uulaa *(jomaa dal oo laa)*
جـمـادى الأولـى

sixth month
jumaadath-thaanii *(jomaa dath thaa nee)*
جـمـادى الـثاني

seventh month
rajab (*rajab*)

رجـب

eighth month
sha`baan (*sha`baan*)

شعـبـان

ninth month
Rama<u>d</u>aan (*rama <u>d</u>aan*)

*رمـضـان

* *Muslims believe that during the month of Rama<u>d</u>aan,*
Allah revealed the first verses of the Qur'an, the holy
book of Islam to the prophet Muhammad. This was
around 610 AD.

Muslims practice <u>s</u>awm, or fasting, for the entire
month of Rama<u>d</u>aan. This means that they abstain from
eating and drinking from sunrise till sunset. During
Rama<u>d</u>aan and in most countries where there is a size-
able number of Muslims, most Muslim restaurants are
closed during the day. Families get up early for su<u>h</u>uur,
a meal eaten before the sun rises. After the sun sets,
the fast is broken with a meal known as if<u>t</u>aar.

tenth month <u>sh</u>awwaal (*<u>sh</u>awwaal*)

*شـوّال

* *Rama<u>d</u>aan ends with a three-day festival of iidd al-fi<u>t</u>r,*
which starts from the first day of <u>sh</u>awwaal. At `iidd al-
fi<u>t</u>r people dress in their best clothes, adorn their homes

with lights and decorations, give treats to children, and exchange visits with friends and family.

eleventh month
dhul qi`dah *(dhol qe` dah)* ذو القعدة

twelfth month
dhuu al-hijjah *(dhol hejjah)* *ذو الحجّة

* *In this month, Muslims perform the* hajj, *the pilgrimage to Mecca in Saudi Arabia, one of the five basic requirements of Islam. Its annual observance corresponds with the major holy day* `iid al-ad-haa, *the second Islamic festival that extends for four days in commemoration of Abraham's readiness to sacrifice his son, Ismael following divine orders.*

While the hajj *is a religious obligation to be fulfilled at least once in each Muslim's lifetime, religious law allows exemption on grounds of hardship or ill-health.*

The hajj *is a series of extensively detailed rituals that include wearing a special garment that symbolizes unity and modesty.*

49 Year

sanah *(sanah)* سـنـة
`aam *(`aam)* عـام

this year
haadhihi as-sanah *(haa dhehes sanah)* هـذه الـسـنـة

last year
as-sanah al-maadiyah *(assanah al maa de yah)*
الـسـنـة الـمـاضـيـة

next year
as-sanah al-qaadimah *(assa nah al qaa demah)*
السـنـة القادمة

every year kul sanah *(kol sanah)* كـل سـنـة

Happy Anniversary!
`aam sa`iid! *(`aam sa `eed!)* عـام سـعـيـد!

New Year's eve
laylat ra's as-sanah *(layy lat ra's assanah)*
لـيـلـة رأس الـسـنـة

Happy New Year!
kul `aam wa anta bi khayr! *(kol `aam wenta bkheir)*
كـل عـام وأنـت بـخـيـر

50 Toilet <u>h</u>ammaam *(<u>h</u>am maam)* حـمّـام

Is there a toilet here?
hal yuujadu <u>h</u>ammaamun hunaa?
(hal yoojado <u>h</u>ammaamon honaa?)
هـل يـوجـد حـمـام هـنا؟

Is there a men's toilet here?
hal yuujadu <u>h</u>ammaam rijaal hunaa?
(hal yoojado <u>h</u>ammaam rejaal honaa?)
هـل يـوجـد حـمـام رجال هـنا؟

Is there a women's toilet here?
hal yuujadu <u>h</u>ammaam sayyidaat hunaa?
(hal yoojado <u>h</u>ammaam sayye datat honaa?)
هـل يـوجـد حـمـام سـيـدات هـنا؟

Where is the toilet, please?
'aynal <u>h</u>ammaamu min fa<u>d</u>lik?
(aynal <u>h</u>ammmaam men fa<u>d</u> lek?)
أيـن الـحـمّـام مـن فـضـلـك؟

Is there a nearby public toilet?
hal yuujadu <u>h</u>ammaamun `umuumiyyun qariibun hunaa? *(hal yoojado <u>h</u>ammaamon `omoomee qaeeeb men honaa?)*
هـل يـوجـد حـمّـام عـمـومـي قـريـب مـن هـنا؟

I need to go to the toilet.
'ahtaaji 'an 'adh-haba 'ilal hammaam
(ahtaajo an adh haba elal hammaam)
أحتاج أن أذهب إلى الحمّام

51 Airport al-mataar *(alma taar)* المطار

To the airport, please.
ilal mataar min fadlik *(elal mataar men fad lek)*
إلى المطار من فضلك

How long does it take to reach the airport?
kam minal waqti nahtaaju linasila ilal mataar?
(kam menal waqte nah taaj lenasela elal mataar?)
كم من الوقت نحتاج لنصل إلى المطار؟

Please meet me at the airport.
qaabilnii fil mataar min fadlik *(qaa belnee fel mataar men fad lek)* قابلني في المطار من فضلك

I will be at the airport.
sa'akuunu fil mataar *(sa akoono fel mataar)*
سأكون في المطار

Will you come to pick me from the airport?
hal sata'tii lita'khudhanii minal mataar?
(hal sata' tee le ta' khodha nee menal mataar?)
هل ستأتي لتأخذني من المطار؟

I will pick you up from the airport.

sa 'aakhudhuka minal maṭaar

(sa aakhodhoka menal maṭaar) سـأخذك مـن المـطـار

I will call you from the airport.

sa 'attaṣilu bika minal maṭaar (sa atta selo beak menal
maṭaar) سـأتـصل بك من المطار

Where is the airport?

'aynal maṭaar? (aynal maṭaar?) أيـن المطـار؟

Is there an international airport?

hal yuujadu maṭaarun dawliyy?

(hal yoojado maṭaaron dawlee?)
هـل يـوجـد مـطـار دولـي؟

52 Taxi sayyarat 'ujrah (sayyaarat ojrah)
سيار ة أجر ة

Taxi! taksii! (tak see!) تكـسي!*

*It's OK to use the English word when you want to stop a
taxi in a street.

I need a taxi.

'aḥtaahu 'ilaa sayyarati ujrah

(aḥ taajo elaa sayyaarate ojrah)
أحـتـاج إلـى سـيـارة أجرة

Please call a taxi for me.
ittasil bisayyarat ujrah law samaht
(ettasel be sayyarate ojrah lao samaht)
اتـصـل بـسـيـارة أجـرة لـو سـمـحـت

I want to go by taxi.
'uriidu 'an 'adh-haba bisayyarati 'ujrah
(oreedo an adh haba be sayyarate ojrah)
أريد أن أذهب بـسـيـارة أجرة

Where can I find a taxi?
'ayna yumkinu 'an 'ajida sayyarat 'ujrah?
(ayna yomkeno an ajeda sayyarata ojrah?)
أين يمكن أن أجد سيارة أجرة؟

How much does it cost to go there by taxi?
kam sayukallifudh dhahaabu 'ilaa hunaak bisayyarati 'ujrah? *(kam sayo kallefodh dhahaabo 'elaa honaak be sayarate ojrah?)*
كـم سيكلف الذهاب إلى هناك بسيارة أجرة؟

Are taxis expensive here?
hal sayyaaraatul 'ujrah muklifah hunaa?
(hal sayyaaratol ojrah moklefaton honaa?)
هـل سيـارات الأجرة مـكـلـفة هـنـا؟

Please call me when the taxi is here.
ittasil bii `indamaa ya'tii saa'iqu sayyaaratil 'ujrah min fadlik *(ettasel bee `endamaa ya' tee saa eqo sayyaaratel ojrah men fad lek)*
بـي عـنـدمـا يـأتـي سـائق سـيـارة الأجرة مـن فضلك

53 Bus

haafilah *(haa felah)* حافلة
* baas (*baas*) باص

* haafilah *is the proper word for "bus" but* baas *is so common that it is OK to be used.*

Is there a nearby bus stop?
hal yuujadu mawqifu baas qariibun min hunaa? *(hal yoojado mawqefo baas qareeb men honaa?)*
هـل يـوجـد مـوقـف بـاص قـريـب مـن هـنـا؟

Where is the bus station?
'ayna mahattatul baasaat? *(ayna mahattatol baasaat?)*
أيـن مـحـطـة الـبـاصـات؟

How can I get to the bus station?
kayfa yumkinunu 'an 'adh-haba 'ilaa mahattatil baasaat? *(kayfa yomkeno an adh haba elaa mahattatel baasaat?)*
كـيـف يـمـكـن أن أذهـب إلـى مـحـطـة الـبـاصـات؟

Which bus should I take to go to Hamidiyya market? (in Damascus)
'ayyu baas yajibu 'an 'aakhudha li'adh-haba ilaa suuq al-hamiidiyyah? *(ayyu baas ya jebo an aa khodha le adh haba elaa sooqel hamee deyyah?)*
أي باص يجب أن آخذ لأذهب إلى سوق الحميدية؟

What is the busfare?
kam ujratul baas?*(kam ojratol baas?)*
كم أجرة الباص؟

Do you have the bus timetable?
hal ladayka jadwal `amalil baasaat?
(hal ladayka jadwalo `amalel baasaat?)
هل لديك جدول عمل الباصات؟

Where does the bus to downtown leave from?
min ayna yantaliqul baasul mutawajjih 'ilaa markazil madiinah? *(men ayna yenta leqol baasol motawajjeho elaa markazel madeenah?)*
من أين ينطلق الباص المتجه إلى مركز المدينة؟

Is there a bus that goes to the airport?
hal hunaaka baas yadh-habu 'ilaa al-mataar?
(hal honaaka baas yadh habo elal mataar?)
هل هناك باص يذهب إلى المطار؟

54 **Train** qitaar *(qetaar)* قطار

Where is the train station?

'ayna mahattatul qitaar? *(ayna mahattatol qetaar?)*

أين محطة القطار؟

I want to go to Cairo by train.

'uriidu 'an 'adh-haba 'ilal qaahirah bil qitaar

(oreedo an adh haba elal qaaherate bel qetaar)

أريد أن أذهب إلى القاهرة بالقطار

Where should I take the train that goes to...?

min 'ayna 'aakhudhul-qitaar mutawajjih ilaa...?

(men ayna akho dhol qetaaral motawajjeha elaa…?)

من أين آخذ القطار المتوجه إلى...؟

How can I get to the train station?

kayfa 'adh-habu 'ilaa mahattatil qitaar?

(kayfa adh habo elaa mahattatel qetaar?)

كيف أذهب إلى محطة القطار؟

Please take me to the train station.

'arjuu 'an ta'khudhanii 'ilaa mahattatil qitaar

(arjoo an ta' khodha nee elaa mahattatel qetaar)

أرجو أن تأخذني إلى محطة القطار

Where can I buy a train ticket?
min ‘ayna yumkinunii ‘an ‘a<u>sh</u>tarii ta<u>dh</u>kirata qi<u>t</u>aar? *(men ayna yomkenonee an a<u>sh</u> taree ta<u>dh</u> kirata qe<u>t</u>aar?)*
مـن أيـن يـمـكـنـنـي أن أشـتـري تـذكـرة قطار؟

How much is the train ticket?
bikam ta<u>dh</u>karatul qi<u>t</u>aar? *(be kam ta<u>dh</u> keratol qe<u>t</u>aar?)*
بـكـم تـذكـرة الـقـطـار؟

55 Hotel funduq *(fondoq)* فـنـدق

To the hotel, please!
‘ilal funduqi min fa<u>d</u>lik *(elal fondoqe men fa<u>d</u>lek)*
إلى الفندق من فضلك

I am staying at a hotel.
‘anaa ‘anzilu fii funduq *(anaa anzelo fee fondoq)*
أنـا أنزل في فندق

We stayed at a hotel.
nazalnaa fii funduq *(nazalnaa fee fondoq)*
نزلنا في فندق

I want to go to my hotel.
‘uriidu ‘an a<u>dh</u>-haba ‘ilal funduq min fa<u>d</u>lik *(oreedo an a<u>dh</u> haba elal fondoq men fa<u>d</u> lek)*
أريد أن أذهب إلى الفندق من فضلك

I want to go to Meridian Hotel.
'uriidu 'an 'adh-haba ila funduqil miridyan
(oreedo an adh haba elaa fondoqel meredyan)
أريد أن أذهب إلى فندق الميريديان

My hotel is ... .
funduqii huwa *(fondoqee howa ... .)* فندقي هو... .

I am looking for a 4-star hotel.
'anaa 'abhathu `an funduqi 'arba`ati nujuum
(anaa ab hatho `an fondoqe arba`ate nojoom)
أنا أبحث عن فندق أربعة نجوم

I don't like this hotel.
laa yu`jubunii haadhal funduq
(laa yo`jebonee haadhal fondoq) لا يعجبني هذا الفندق

Meet me at the hotel.
qaabilnii fil funduq *(qaa belnee fel fondoq)*
قابلني في الفندق

I want to go to another hotel.
'uriidu 'an 'araa funduqan 'aakhar *(oreedo an araa fondoqan aakhar)* أريد أن أرى فندقاً آخر

See you at the hotel.
'araaka fil funduq *(araaka fel fondoq)* أراك في الفندق

56 Home bayt *(bayyt)* بيت

This is my home.

haa<u>dh</u>aa baytii *(haa <u>dh</u>aa bayytee)* هذا بيتي

This is a nice home.

haa<u>dh</u>aa baytun jamiil *(haa<u>dh</u>aa bayton jameel)*
هذا بيت جميل

I am staying at my friend's home.

'ana 'anzilu fii bayti <u>s</u>adiiqii
(anaa anzelo fee bayte <u>s</u>adeeqee)
أنا أنزل في بيت صديقي

I am home.

ana fil bayt *(anaa fel bayt)* أنــا في البيت

Where is your home?

'ayna baytuk? *(ayna baytok?)* أين بيتك؟

Is your home in this suburb?

hal baytuka fii haa<u>dh</u>ihi<u>d</u> <u>d</u>aa<u>h</u>iyah?
(hal baytoka fee haa<u>dh</u>ehe<u>d</u> <u>d</u>aa <u>h</u>eyah?)
هـل بيتك في هذه الضـاحية؟

Meet me at my home.

qaabilnii fii baytii *(qaabelnee fee baytee)*
قابلني في بيتي

Who lives in this house?

man yaskunu fii haa<u>dh</u>al bayt?

(man yaskono fee haa<u>dh</u>al bayt?)

من يسكن في هذا البيت؟

57 Street shaari` *(shaa re`)* شـارع

What is this street called?

masmu haa<u>dh</u>a<u>sh</u> shaari`? *(masmo haa <u>dh</u>a<u>sh</u> share`?)*

ما اسم هذا الشارع؟

I live on ... Street.

'askunu fii <u>sh</u>arI` ... *(askono fee share` ...)*

أسكن في شارع ...

I like this street because it is full of shops.

yu`jibunii haa<u>dh</u>a<u>sh</u> <u>sh</u>aari` li'annahu malii'un bel
ma<u>h</u>allaatit tijaariyyah *(yo`jebo nee haa <u>dh</u>a<u>sh</u> shaare`
le annaho malee on bel ma<u>h</u>allaatet tejaa reyyah)*

يعجبني هذا الشارع لأنه مليء بالمحلات التجارية

Is ... Street far from here?

hal <u>sh</u>aari`u ... ba`iid? *(hal <u>sh</u>aa re`o ... ba`eed?)*

هل شارع ... بعيد؟

58 Hairdresser's Shop

qaa`at <u>h</u>ilaaqah *(qaa `at <u>h</u>elaa qah)*
قـاعــة حلاقــة

Is there a nearby hairdresser?
hal yuujadu qaa`at <u>h</u>ilaaqah?
(hal yoojado qaa`ato <u>h</u>elaaqah qareebah?)
هل يوجد قاعة حلاقة قريبة من هنا؟

I want to go to the hairdresser's.
'uriidu 'an 'a<u>dh</u>-haba 'ilaa qaa`ati <u>h</u>ilaaqah
(oreedo an a<u>dh</u> haba elaa qaa`ate <u>h</u>elaaqah)
أريد أن أذهب إلى قاعة حلاقة

Is there another hairdresser?
hal yuujadu qaa`atu <u>h</u>ilaaqatin 'u<u>kh</u>raa?
(hal yoojado qaa`ato <u>h</u>elaaqaten o<u>kh</u> raa?)
هل يوجد قاعة حلاقة أخرى؟

59 Bar <u>h</u>aanah (*<u>h</u>aanah*) حـانــة

Where is the bar?
'aynal <u>h</u>aanah? *(aynal <u>h</u>aanah?)* أين الحانة؟

What is the nearest bar?
'ayna 'aqrab <u>h</u>aanah? *(ayna aqrab <u>h</u>aanah?)*
أين أقرب حانة؟

I want to go to a bar.
'uriidu 'an 'adh-haba 'ilal haanah
(oreedo an adh haba elal haanah)
أريد أن أذهب إلى الحانة

This is a nice bar.
haadhihil haanah jayyidah
(haa dhehel haanah jayyedah) هذه الحانة جيدة

I like this bar.
tu`jibunii haadhihil haanah
(to`jebo nee haa dhehel haanah) تعجبني هذه الحانة

I don't like this bar.
haadhihil haanah laa tu`jibunii
(haa dhehel haanah laa to` jebonee)
هذه الحانة لا تعجبني

Meet me at the bar.
qaabilnii fil haanah *(qaabel nee fel haanah)*
قابلني في الحانة

I will be at the bar.
sa'akuunu fil haanah *(sa akoono fel haanah)*
سأكون في الحانة

60 Night club naadii layliyy *(naadee laylee)*

نــادي لــيـلــيّ

Where is the night club?

'aynan naadil layliyy? *(aynan naadel laylee?)*

أين النــادي لــيـلــي ؟

What is the nearest night club?

'ayna 'aqrab naadin layliyy?

(ayna aqrab naaden laylee?) أين أقرب نــادي لــيـلــيّ ؟

I want to go to a night club.

'uriidu 'an 'adh-haba 'ilan naadil layliyy

(oreedo an adh haba elan naadel laylee)

أريد أن أذهب إلى النــادي لــيـلــيّ

This is a good night club.

haadhan naadil layliyy jayyid *(haa dhaa naaden laylee jayyed)* هذا النــادي لــيـلــيّ جيد

I like this night club.

yu`jibunii haadhan naadil layliyy *(yo`jebo nee haa dhan naadel laylee)* يعجبني هذا النادي الليلي

I don't like this night club.

haadhan naadil layliyy laa yu`jibunii *(haadhan naadel laylee laa yo` jebonee)* هذا النادي الليلي لا يعجبني

Meet me at the night club.
qaabilnii fin naadil layliyy *(qaabel nee fen naadel laylee)* قابلني في النادي الليلي

61 Zoo <u>h</u>adiiqat <u>h</u>ayawaan
(<u>h</u>adee qat <u>h</u>aya waan) حديقة حيوان

Is there a zoo in this city?
hal yuujadu <u>h</u>adiiqat <u>h</u>ayawaan fii haa<u>dh</u>ihil madiinah? *(hal yoo jado <u>h</u>a dee qato hayawaa fee haa <u>dh</u>ehel madeenah?)*
هل يوجد حديقة حيوان في هذه المدينة؟

Take me to the zoo, please.
<u>kh</u>u<u>dh</u>nii ‘ilaa <u>h</u>adiiqatil <u>h</u>ayawaan law sama<u>h</u>t
(<u>kh</u>o<u>dh</u> nee elaa <u>h</u>adee qatel <u>h</u>ayawaan lao sama<u>h</u>t)
خذني إلى حديقة الحيوان لو سمحت

I want to go to the zoo.
‘uriidu ‘anm ‘a<u>dh</u> haba ‘ilaa <u>h</u>adiiqatil <u>h</u>ayawaan
(oreedo an a<u>dh</u> haba elaa <u>h</u>adee qatel <u>h</u>ayawaan)
أريد أن أذهب إلى حديقة الحيوان

I'm at the zoo.
‘anaa fii <u>h</u>adiiqatil <u>h</u>ayawaan
(anaa fee <u>h</u>adee qatel <u>h</u>ayawaan) أنا في حديقة الحيوان

Let's go to the zoo!

falna<u>dh</u>-hab ilaa <u>h</u>adiiqatil <u>h</u>ayawaan! (*fal na<u>dh</u> hab elaa <u>h</u>adee qatel <u>h</u>ayawaan!*) فلنذهب إلى حديقة الحيوان!

62 Letters & Post Office

risaalah wa maktab bariid (*resaalah wa maktab bareed*)

رسالة ومـكـتـب بـريـد

I want to send a letter.

'uriidu 'an 'ursila risaalah (*oreedo an orsela resaalah*)

أريد أن أرسل رسالة

I will send you a letter.

sa'ursilu laka risaalah (*sa orselo laka resaalah*)

سأرسل لك رسالة

Is there any letter for me?

hal yuujadu ayyatu risaalatin lii?

(*hal yoojado ayyato resaalaten lee?*)

هل يوجد أية رسالة لي؟

I received a letter.

istalamtu risaalah (*esta lamto resaalah*) استلمت رسالة

I didn't receive any letter.

lam astalim ayyat risaalah

(*lam astalem ayyat resaalah*) لم أستلم أية رسالة

Where is the nearest post office?
'ayna 'aqrabu maktabu bariid?
(ayna aqrabo maktabe bareed?)
أيـن أقـرب مـكـتـب بـريـد؟

How do I get to the post office?
kayfa 'asilu 'ilaa maktabil bariid?
(kayfa aselo elaa mak table bareed?)
كـيـف أصـل إلـى مـكـتـب الـبـريـد؟

63 Famous Meals

aklaat mash-huurah *(ak laat mash hoorah)*
أكـلات مـشـهـورة

Meat or chicken served on rice
kabsah *(kabsah)* كـبـسـة

Fried eggplant, potato, onion, tomato and nuts cooked and served on rice
maqluubaa *(maq loo bah)* مـقـلـوبـة

Lamb seasoned in aromatic herbs and cooked in dry yoghurt "jamiid," then served on rice
mansaf *(mansaf)* مـنـسـف

Bread with onion, olive oil, saffron, nuts, and grilled chicken
msakh-khan *(m sakh khan)* مـسـخـن

Rice with fried or grilled fish
s̲ayyadiyya *(s̲ayyaa deyyah)* صـيـاديـة

Vegetables stuffed with minced meat and rice
dulma *(dol maa)* دولـمـا

Rice, lentil, onion and spices mixed together and fried
kus̲h̲arii *(ko s̲h̲a ree)* كـشـري

Couscous, onion, meat, potato, chickpea, butter, saffron and olive oil
kusksii *(kosk see)* كـسـكـسـي

Eggplant, vine leaves and /or zucchini stuffed with rice and minced meat in a tomato sauce
mah̲s̲h̲ii *(mah s̲h̲ee)* مـحـشـي

Lamb chops, green beans and onion cooked in tomato soup and served with rice
fas̲uulyaa k̲h̲ad̲raa *(faa s̲ool yaa k̲h̲ad̲ raa)*
فـاصـولـيـا خـضـرا

Raw oval-shaped nuggets of minced lamb and burghul "kibbi," eaten like steak tartar
kibbi nayyi *(keb beh nayye)* كـبـة نـيـة

Trimmed okra, lamb chops, garlic and olive oil cooked in tomato soup and served with rice
baamyaa *(baam yaa)* بـــامـــيـــة

64 Newspaper & Magazine

jariidah wa majallah *(jaree dah wa ma jal lah)*
جريدة ومجلة

Do you have today's newspaper?
hal `indaka jariidatul yawm?
(hal `endaka jaree datol yaom?) هل عندك جريدة اليوم؟

I want to read the newspaper.
'uriidu 'an 'aqra'al jariidah
(oreedo an aqra al jaree dah) أريد أن أقرأ الجريدة

How much is this magazine?
bikam haa<u>dh</u>ihil majallah?
(bekam haa <u>dh</u>ehel majal lah?) بكم هذه المجلة؟

I would like to buy this magazine.
'awaddu 'an 'a<u>sh</u>tarii haa<u>dh</u>ihil majallah
(awaddo an a<u>sh</u> taree haa <u>dh</u>ehel majal lah)
أودّ أن أشـتـري هـذه الـمـجـلـة

Do you have English newspapers?
hal `indaka jaraa'idun bil-inkliiziyyah?
(hal `endaka jaraa edon bel eng lee zeyyah?)
هل عندك جرائد بالإنجليزية؟

Do you have English magazines?
hal `indaka majallaatun bil-inkliiziyyah?
(hal `endaka majal laa ton bel eng lee zeyyah?)
هل عندك مجلات بالإنجليزية؟

Where can I buy a newspaper?
'ayna yumkinunii 'an 'ashtarii jariidah?
(ayna yomkenonee an ash taree jaree dah?)
أين يمكنني أن أشتري جريدة؟

65 Radio idhaa`ah *(edhaa `ah)* إذاعة

Turn the radio on, please.
shagh-ghilil midhyaa` min fadlik
(shagh ghel al medh yaa` men fad lek)
شغل المذياع من فضلك

Turn the radio off, please.
atfi' midhyaa` min fadlik
(atfi' al medh yaa` men fad lek) أطفئ المذياع من فضلك

Put the radio volume up, please.
irfa` sawtal midhyaa` min fadlik *(erfa` sawtal medh yaa` men fad lek)* ارفع صوت المذياع من فضلك

Put the radio volume down, please.
akhfid sawtal midhyaa` min fadlik *(akh fed sawtal medh yaa` men fad lek)* اخفض صوت المذياع من فضلك

What is this radio station called?
masmu haadhihil mahattatil idhaa`iyyah?
(masmo haa dhehel mahatta tel edhaa `eyyah?)
ما اسم هذه المحطة الإذاعية؟

I am listening to the radio.
'anaa 'astami`u 'ilal 'idhaa`ah
(anaa asta me`o elal edhaa `ah) أنا أستمع إلى الإذاعة

I like listening to the radio.
'uhibbul istimaa`a ilal 'idhaa`ah *(ohebbol estemaa`a elal edhaa `ah)* أحب الاستماع إلى الإذاعة

I don't listen to the radio that much.
laa 'astami`u 'ilal 'idhaa`ati kathiiran *(laa asta me`o elal edhaa `ate kathee ran)* لا أستمع إلى الإذاعة كثيراً

I want to buy a radio.
'uriidu 'an 'ashtarii midhyaa`
(oreedo an ashta ree medh yaa`) أريد أن أشتري مذياع

66 TV tilfaaz *(tel faaz)* تــلــفــاز

Turn the TV on, please.

sha<u>gh</u> <u>gh</u>il attilfaaz min fa<u>d</u>lik *(shagh ghel attel faaz men fad lek)* شغل التلفاز من فضلك

Is there a TV in the room?

hal yuujadu tilfaaz fil <u>gh</u>urfah? *(hal yoojado telfaaz fel ghorfah?)* هل يوجد تلفاز في الغرفة؟

I want to buy a TV.

'uriidu 'an 'a<u>sh</u>tariya tilfaaz *(oreedo an ashta ree tel faaz)* أريد أن أشتري تلفاز

Are there English channels on the TV?

hal hunaaka ma<u>h</u>a<u>tt</u>atun tilfizyuuniyyah inkliiziyyah? *(hal honaaka mahattaa ton tel fez yoo neyyah englee zeyyah?)* هل هناك محطات تلفزيونية إنجليزية؟

I am watching TV.

'anaa 'i<u>sh</u>aahidut tilfaaz *(anaa oshaa hedot tel faaz)* أنا أشاهد التلفاز

I will be watching TV.

sa'akuunu 'u<u>sh</u>aahidut tilfaaz *(sa akoono oshaa hedot tel faaz)* سأكون أشاهد التلفاز

I watched TV yesterday.

shaahadtut tilfaaz ams *(shaa hadtot tel faaz ams)*

شاهدت التلفاز أمس

I saw it on TV.

ra'aytuhu fit tilfaaz *(ra ayto ho fet tel faaz)*

رأيته في التلفاز

67 Phone haatif *(haa tef)* هاتف

Can I use the telephone, please?

hal yumkinunii 'an 'astakhdimal haatif min fadlik?

(hal yomkenonee an astakh demal haatefa men fad lek?)

هل يمكنني أن أستخدم الهاتف من فضلك؟

I want to make a phone call.

'uriidu 'an 'ujrii mukaalamah haatifiyyah

(oreedo an ojree mokaalamah haa tefeyyah)

أريد أن أجرى مكالمة هاتفية

What is your phone number?

maa raqmu haatifika? *(maa raqmo haa tefeka?)*

ما رقم هاتفك؟

This is my phone number.

haadhaa huwa raqmu haatifii

(haa dhaa howa raqmo haa tefee) هذا هو رقم هاتفي

Write your phone number here.
sajjil raqma haatifika hunaa
(sajjel raqma haa tefeka honaa) سجل رقم هاتفك هنا

Is there a phone here?
hal yuujadu haatifun hunaa?
(hal yoojado haa tefon honaa?) هل يوجد هاتف هنا؟

I want to make an international phone call.
'uriidu 'an 'ujrii mukaalamah haatifiyyah dawliyyah
(oreedo an ojree mokaalamah haa tefeyyah daw-leyyah) أريـد أن أجري هاتفية دولية

68 Mobile phone jawwaal *(jawwaal)* جوال*

* Other terms for "mobile phones" might be

haatif ma<u>h</u>muul *(haatef ma<u>h</u> mool)* هاتف محمول

naqqaal *(naqqaal)* نقال

<u>kh</u>alawiyy *(<u>kh</u>alawee)* خلوي

Is this your mobile phone?
hal haa<u>dh</u>aa jawwaaluk? *(hal haa<u>dh</u>aa jawwaalok?)*
هل هذا جوالك؟

I have a mobile phone.
`indii jawwaal *(`endee jawwaal)* عندي جوال

I don't have a mobile phone.
laysa `indii jawwaal *(laysa `endee jawwaal)*
ليس عندي جوال

Do you have a mobile phone?
hal `indaka jawwaal? *(hal `endaka jawwaal?)*
هل عندك جوال؟

What's your mobile number?
maa raqmu jawwaalik? *(maa raqmo jawwaalek?)*
ما رقم جوالك؟

Please write down my mobile number.
sajjil raqma jawwaalii *(sajjel raqma jawwaalee)*
سجل رقم جوالي

I like your mobile phone.
jawwaaluka yu`jibunii *(jawwaaloka yo` jebonee)*
جوالك يعجبني

I want to buy a mobile phone.
'uriidu 'an 'a<u>sh</u>tariya jawwaal
(oreedo an a<u>sh</u>tareeya jawwaal) أريد أن أشتري جوال

I want to repair my mobile phone.
‘uriidu ‘an ‘usalliha jawwaalii
(oreedo an osalleha jawwaalee) أريد أن أصلح جوالي

69 Call yattasil *(yatta sel)* يتصل

Call me please.
ittasil bii min fadlik *(ettasel bee men fad lek)*
اتصل بي من فضلك

I will call you.
sawfa attasilu bik *(sawfa attaselo bek)* سوف أتصل بك

I didn’t call.
lamm ‘attasil *(lamm atta sel)* لم أتصل

Did you call?
halit tasalta? *(halet tasalta?)* هل اتصلت؟

Did anyone call me?
halit tasala ahadun bii? *(halet tasala ahadon bee?)*
هل اتصل أحد بى؟

Have you called them yet?
alam tattasil bihim ba`d? *(alam tatta sel behem ba`d?)*
ألم تتصل بهم بعد؟

Call the police.
ittasil bish shurtah *(ettasel besh shortah)*
اتصل بالشرطة

Call an ambulance.
ittasil bil ‘is`aaf *(etta sel bel es `aaf)* اتصل بالإسعاف

Call a taxi.
‘utlub sayyaarata ‘ujrah (otlob sayyaarata ojrah)
أطلب سيارة أجرة

70 Computer haasuub *(haasoob)* حاسوب

I need a computer.
‘ahtaaju ilaa haasuub *(ahtaajo elaa haasoob)*
أحتاجُ إلى حاسوب

May I use your computer?
hal yumkinunii ‘an ‘astakhdima haasuubak?
(hal yomkenonee an astakh dema haasoobak?)
هل يمكِنني أن أستخدِم حاسوبك؟

How can I switch this keyboard to English?
kayfa yumkinunii ‘an ‘uhawwila haadhal haasuub ‘ilal inkliiziyyah? *(kayfa yomkeno an ohawwela haa dhal haasoob elal engleezeyyah?)*
كيف يمكن أن أحوّل هذا الحاسوب إلى
الإنجليزية؟

I want to repair my laptop.

'uriidu 'an 'usalliha haasuubil mahmuul

(oreedo an osalleha haasoobel mahmool)

أريد أن أصلح حاسوبي المحمول

Where is the nearest computer shop?

ayna aqrabu mahalli hawasiib?

(ayna aqrabo mahalle hawaseeb?)

أين أقرب محل حواسيب؟

71 Internet & E-mail

'intirnit wa bariid iliktrunitt

(enter net wa bareed elek tronee)

إنــتــرنــت وبــريــد إلــكــتــرونــي

I would like to check my e-mail, please.

'awaddu 'an 'uraaji`a bariidil 'iliktruniyy *(awaddo an oraa je`a bareedel elek tronee)*

أود أن أراجــع بــريــدي الإلــكــتــرونــي

Is the internet available here?

hal yuujadu intirnit hunaa?

(hal yoojado enter net honaa?) هل يوجد إنترنت هنا؟

Can I use the internet?

hal yumkinunii 'an 'astakhdimal intirnit?

(hal yomkeno nee an astakh demal enter net?)

هل يمكنني أن أستخدم الإنترنت؟

Where can I go to use the internet?
'ayna yumkinu 'an a'<u>dh</u>-haba li asta`milal 'intirnit? *(ayna yomkeno an a<u>dh</u> haba le asta` melal enter net?)* أيـن يـمـكـن أن أذهـب لأسـتـعـمـل الإنـتـرنـت؟

In there an internet café?
hal yuujadu maqhaa 'intirnit? *(hal yoojado maqhaa enter net?)* هـل يـوجـد مـقـهـى إنـتـرنـت؟

I want to search the internet for … .
'uriidu 'an 'ab<u>h</u>a<u>th</u>a fil 'intirnit `an … . *(oreedo an ab<u>h</u>a<u>th</u>a fel enter net `an)* أريـد أن أبـحـث فـي الإنـتـرنـت عـن… .

How much is the usage per hour?
kam 'ujratul intirnit fis saa`ah? *(kam ojratol enter net fes saa`ah?)* كـم أجـرة الإنترنت فـي الـسـاعـة؟

What is your e-mail address?
maa huwa bariidukal 'iliktruniyy? *(maa howa baree-dokal elek troonee?)* مـا هـو بـريـدك الإلـكـتـرونـي؟

72 **Seasons** al-fu<u>s</u>uul *(alfo <u>s</u>ool)* الـفـصـول

season fa<u>s</u>l *(fasl)* فـصـل

winter <u>sh</u>itaa' *(<u>sh</u>etaa')* شـتـاء

spring rabii` (_rabee`_) ربيع

summer ṣayf (_ṣayf_) صيف

autumn ḵhariif (_ḵhareef_) خريف

What is the best season in Syria?

maa huwa afḏalul fuṣuul fii suuryaa?
(_maa howa af ḏalol foṣool fee sooryaa_)
مـا هـو أفـضـل الـفـصول فـي سـوريـا؟

When does summer begin?

mataa yabda'u fasluṣ-ṣayf? (_mataa yabda o faslos ṣayf?_)
مـتـى يـبـدأ فصل الصـيـف؟

Is it very cold during winter?

haliṭ ṭaqṣu* baaridun jiddan fiṣh-ṣhitaa'?
(_haleṭ ṭaqṣo baa redon jeddan feṣh ṣhetaa'?_)
هـل الطـقـس بـارد جداً في الـشـتـاء؟

* _ṭaqṣ_ means "weather" and is mostly mentioned in the
  question "Is the weather cold?," not "Is it cold?" as in
  English.

What is the maximum temperature in Riyadh?

maa hiya darajatul ḥaraaratil quṣwaa fir riyaaḏ?
(_maa heya da rajatol ḥaraa ratel qoṣwaa fer reyaaḏ?_)
مـا هـي درجـة الـحـرارة الـقـصـوى فـي الـريـاض؟

73 Weather

aljaww *(aljao)* الجو
at̲ t̲aqs *(at̲ t̲aqs)* الطقس

What is the weather like today?
kayfa huwa at̲-t̲aqs al-yawm? *(kayfa howat̲ t̲aq sol yaom?)* كـيـف هـو الـطـقـس الـيـوم؟

What will the weather be like tomorrow?
kayfa sayakuunut̲ t̲aqsu g̲h̲adan? *(kayfa saya koonot̲ t̲aqso g̲h̲adan?)* كيف سيكون الطقس غداً؟

I don't like humid weather.
laa uh̲ibbul jawwar rat̲ib *(laa oh̲ebbol jawwar rat̲eb)* لا أحـب الـجـوّ الـرطـب

The weather is lovely here.
aljawwu jamiilun alyawm
(aljawwo jamee lon alyawm) الجو جميل اليوم

I like the weather here.
aljawwo hunaa yu`jibunii *(aljawwo honaa yo` jebonee)* الجو هنا يعجبني

I don't like the weather here.
aljawwu hunaa laa yu`jibunii *(aljawwo honaa laa yo` jebonee)* الجو هنا لا يعجبني

Did you read the weather forecast?
hal qara'tan nashratal jawwiyyah? *(hal qara' tan nash ratal jawweyyah?)* هل قرأت النشرة الجوية؟

74 Hot haarr *(haa rr)* حار

The weather is hot today.
aljawwu haarrun alyawm *(aljawwo haarron al yaom)*
الجو حار اليوم

Will it be hot tomorrow?
hal sayakuunul jawwu haarran ghadan?
(hal saya koonol jawwo haarran ghadan?)
هل سيكون الجو حاراً غداً؟

It was hot yesterday.
kanal jawwu haarran ams
(ka anal jawwo haarran ams) كان الجو حاراً أمس

I don't like hot weather.
laa 'uhibbut taqsal haarr *(laa ohebbot taqsal haa rr)*
لا أحب الطقس الحار

Is it always hot here?
halil jawwu haarrun daa'iman hunaa?
(halel jawwo haarron daa eman honaa?)
هل الجو حار دائماً هنا؟

Do you like hot weather?

hal tuhibbut taqsal haarr? *(hal tohebbot taqsal haa rr?)*
هل تحب الطقس الحار؟

The food is too hot/spicy.

atta`aamu haarrun jiddan *(atta `aamo haarron jeddan)*
الطعام حار جداً

Is there hot water?

hal yuujadu maa'un haarr?
(hal yoo jado maa on haa rr?) هل يوجد ماء حار؟

75 Cold baarid *(baa red)* بارد

The weather is cold today.

aljawwu baaridun alyawm
(aljawwo baa redon al yawm) الجو بارد اليوم

Will it be cold tomorrow?

hal sayakuunul jawwu baaridan ghadan?
(hal saya koonol jawwo baa redan ghadan?)
هل سيكون الجو بارداً عذاً؟

It was cold yesterday.

kanal jawwu baaridan ams
(ka anal jawwo baa redan ams) كان الجو بارداً أمس

I don't like cold weather.
laa 'u<u>h</u>ibbu<u>t</u> <u>t</u>aqsal <u>h</u>aarr *(laa o<u>h</u>ebbo<u>t</u> <u>t</u>aqsal <u>h</u>aa rr)*
لا أحب الطقس البارد

Is it always cold here?
halil jawwu baaridun daa'iman hunaa? *(halel jawwo baa redon daa eman honaa?)* هل الجو بارد دائماً هنا؟

Do you like cold weather?
hal tu<u>h</u>ibbu<u>t</u> <u>t</u>aqsal baarid?
(hal to<u>h</u>ebbo<u>t</u> <u>t</u>aqsal baa red?) هل تحب الطقس البارد؟

The food is too cold.
a<u>tt</u>a`aamu baarid jiddan *(a<u>tt</u>a `aamo baa red jeddan)*
الطعام بارد جداً

Is there cold water?
hal yuujadu maa'un baarid?
(hal yoo jado maa on baa red?) هل يوجد ماء بارد؟

76 Too / Very jiddan *(jed dan)* جِـــدّاً

This is very expensive.
<u>h</u>aa<u>dh</u>aa <u>gh</u>aalin jiddan
(haa <u>dh</u>aa <u>gh</u>aa len jeddan) هذا غالٍ جداً

The weather is too hot for us to walk.
aljawwu haarrun jiddan hatta namshii *(aljawwo haar-ron jeddan hatta namshee)* الجو حار جداً حتى نمشي

It is very cold.
aljawwu baaridun jiddan *(aljawwo baa redon jeddan)*
الجو بارد جداً

I am very tired.
'anaa ta`baan jiddan *(anaa ta` baan jeddan)*
أنا تعبان جداً

It is very delicious.
innahaa ladhiidhatun jiddan
(enna haa ladhee dhaton jeddan) إنها لذيذة جداً

You are very beautiful.
'anti jamiilatun jiddan *(ante jamee laton jeddan)*
أنت جميلة جداً

It is very far.
'innahaa ba`iidatun jiddan
(ennahaa ba`ee daton jeddan) إنها بعيدة جداً

This hotel is very clean.
haadhal funduq naziifun jiddan
(haa dhal fondoq nazee fon jeddan)
هذا الفندق نظيف جداً

77 **Student** ṯaalib *(ṯaaleb)* طـالـب

I am a student. (*male*)
'anaa ṯaalib *(anaa ṯaaleb)* أنا طالب

I am a student. (*female*)
'anaa ṯaalibah *(anaa ṯaalebah)* أنـا طـالـبـة

We are students.
naẖnu ṯullaab *(naẖno ṯollaab)* نحن طلاب

Are you a student?
hal anta ṯaalib? *(hal anta ṯaa leb?)* هل أنت طالب؟

I am staying in a students' dormitory.
'anaa 'askunu fii sakaniṯ ṯullaab *(anaa askono fee saka neṯ ṯollaab)* أنا أسكن فى سكن الطلاب

I am a university student.
'anaa ṯaalib fil jaami`ah *(anaa ṯaaleb fel jaa me `ah)* أنا طالب في الجامعة

I am a high-school student.
'anaa ṯaalib fi<u>th</u> <u>th</u>aanawiyyah
(anaa ṯaaleb fe<u>th</u> <u>th</u>aa naweyyah) أنا طالب في الثانوية

My son is a student.
ibnii ṯaalib *(eb nee ṯaaleb)* ابني طالب

Here is my student card.
haadhihi hiya bitaaqatii al-jaami`iyyah
(haa dhe he heya be taaqatel jaa me `eyyah)
هـذه هـي بـطـاقـتي الـجـامـعـيـة

Is there a student discount?
hal hunaaka khasmun lit-tullaab *(hal honaaka khas mon let tollaab?)* هـل هـنـاك خـصـمٌ لـلـطـلاب؟

78 **Book** kitaab *(ketaab)* كتاب

Have you read a good book lately?
hal qara'ta kitaaban jayyidan mu'akh kharan?
(hal qara'ta ketaaban jayyedan mo akh kharan?)
هل قرأت كتاباً جيداً مؤخراً؟

I am reading an interesting book.
'anaa 'aqra'u kitaaban jayyidan
(anaa aqra o ketaaban jayyedan) أنا أقرأ كتاباً جيداً

I like this book.
yu'jibunii haadhal kitaab
(yo`je bonee haa dhal ketaab) يعجبني هذا الكتاب

Is there a nearby bookstore?
hal yuujadu maktabatun qariibah? *(hal yoo jado mak tabaton qareebah?)* هل يوجد مكتبة قريبة؟

I would like to buy this book.

'awaddu 'an 'ashtarii haadhal kitaab

(awaddo an ash taree haa dhal ketaab)

أود أن أشتري هذا الكتاب

How much is this book?

bikam haadhal kitaab? *(bekam haa dhal ke tab?)*

بكم هذا الكتاب؟

I want to buy a book about Egypt.

'uriidu 'an 'ashtariya kitaaban `an misr

(oreedo an ash tareya ketaaban `an mesr)

أريـد أن أشـتـري كـتـابـاً عـن مـصـر

I want to buy a book on the Arabic language.

'uriidu 'an 'ashtariya kitaaban `anil lughatil `arabiyyah

(oreedo an ash tareya ketaaban `anel logha tel `ara beyyah)

أريـد أن أشـتـري كـتـابـاً عـن الـلـغـة الـعـربـيـة

Where can I find information books?

'ayna yumkinunii 'an ajida kutuban irshaadiyyah?

(ayna yomkenonee an ajeda kotoban er shaa deyyah?)

أيـن يـمـكـنـنـي أن أجـد كـتـبـاً إرشـاديـة؟

79 Money

nuquud *(noqood)* نقود
maal *(maal)* مال

I don't have cash.
laysa `indii naqd *(laysa `endee naqd)* ليس عندي نقد

Do you have enough money?
hal `indaka maalun kaafii *(hal `endaka maalon kaafee?)*
هل عندك مال كافٍ؟

I don't have enough money.
laysal `indil maalul kaafii *(laysa `endel maalol kaafee)*
ليس عندي المال الكافي

Is it safe to carry cash ?
hal minal 'aamin 'an 'ahmila naqdan?
(hal menal aamen an ah mela naqdan?)
هل من الآمن أن أحمل نقداً؟

I left my money at the hotel.
taraktu nuquudii fil fonduq
(tarakto noqoodee fel fon doq) تركت نقودي في الفندق

I lost my money.
laqad ada`tu nuquudii *(laqad ada`to noqoodee)*
لقد أضعت نقودي

Do you need money?

hal ta<u>h</u>taaju maalan? *(hal ta<u>h</u> taajo maalan?)*

هل تحتاج مالاً؟

I need some money.

'a<u>h</u>taaju ba`<u>d</u>al maal

(ah taajo ba` <u>d</u>al maal) أحتاج بعض المال

How much money do you need?

kam minal maali ta<u>h</u>taaj? *(kam menal maal ta<u>h</u> taaj?)*

كم من المال تحتاج؟

80 Work ya`mal *(ya`mal)* يعمل

Where do you work?

'ayna ta`mal? *(ayna ta`mal?)* أيـن تـعـمـل؟

I work in ... .

'anaa 'a`malu fii … . *(anaa a`malo fee… .)*

أنـا أعـمـل فـي ....

Do you work here?

hal ta`malu hunaa? *(hal ta`malo honaa?)* هل تعمل هنا؟

I don't work here.

'anaa laa 'a`malu hunaa *(anaa laa a`malo honaa)*

أنا لا أعمل هنا

I work in France.
'anaa 'a`malu fii faransaa *(anaa a`malo fee faran saa)*
أنا أعمل في فرنسا

I was at work.
kuntu fil `amal *(konto fel `amal)* كنت في العمل

I am here on a professional visit.
'anaa hunaa fii ziyaarati `amal *(anaa honaa fee zeyaa rate `amal)* أنا هنا في زيارة عمل

I was working there a long time ago.
kuntu 'a`malu hunaak qabla qa`tin ṯawiil
(konto a`malo honaak qabla qa` ten ṯaw eel)
كنت أعمل هناك قبل وقت طويل

81 Meeting ijtimaa` *(ej temaa`)* اجتماع

I was in a meeting.
kuntu fii ijtimaa` *(konto fee ej temaa`)* كنت في اجتماع

I have an important meeting.
`indii ijtimaa`un muhim *(`endee ejtemaa`on mohem)*
عندي اجتماع مهم

I will be at the meeting.
sa'akuunu fil ijtimaa` *(sa akoonoi fel ej temaa`)*
سأكون في الاجتماع

It was a long meeting.
kaanaj timaa`an tawiilan *(kaanaj temaa `an taweelan)*
كان اجتماعاً طويلاً

I will arrive in time for the meeting.
sa'asilu 'ilal ijtimaa` fil waqtil munaasib
(sa aselo elal ej temaa` fel waqtel monaaseb)
سأصل إلى الاجتماع في الوقت المناسب

I arrived late for the meeting.
wasltu muta'akh khiran ilal ijtimaa` *(was alto mota akh kheran elal ej temaa`)* وصلت متأخراً إلى الاجتماع

Where is the meeting room?
'ayna ghurfatul ijtimaa`aat?
(ayna ghurfatol ej temaa `aat?) أين غرفة الاجتماعات؟

When does the meeting start?
mataa yabda'ul ijtimaa`?
(mataa yab da ol ej temaa`?) متى يبدأ الاجتماع؟

82 Meet

yuqaabil *(yoqaa bel)* يقابل
yaltaqii *(yal taqee)* يلتقي

I would like to meet you.
'awaddu 'an 'uqaabilaka
(awaddo an oqaa belaka) أود أن أقابلك

I will meet Mark tomorrow.
sa'uqaabilu maark ghadan
(sa oqaabelo maark gha dan) سأقابل مارك غداً

I am not going to meet him.
lan 'altaqiya bih *(lan alta qeya beh)* لن ألتقي به

Will you meet me?
hal sataltaqii bii? *(hal sat al taqee bee?)* هل ستلتقي بي؟

I met Sandra.
qaabaltu saandraa *(qaa balto saan draa)* قابلت ساندرا

I didn't meet Peter.
lam 'altaqi biitir *(lam al taqe bee ter)* لم ألتق بيتر

Let's meet at 11 a.m.!
fal naltaqis saa`atal haadiyata `ashtarah!
(fal nal taqes saa `atal haa deyata `ash tarah!)
فلنلتق الساعة الحادية عشرة!

Where shall we meet?
'ayna sanaltaqii? *(ayna sa nalta qee?)* أين سنلتقي؟

Meet me at the hotel.
qaabilnii fil funduq *(qaa bel nee fel fon doq)*
قابلني في الفندق

83 Market & Shopping

market: suuq *(sooq)* ســوق

shopping: tasawwuq *(ta sawwoq)* تسوق

I want to go shopping.

'uriidu 'an atasawwaq *(oreedo an ata sawwaq)*

أريد أن أتسوق

Let's go shopping!

falna<u>dh</u> hab littasawwuq!

(fal na<u>dh</u> hab let tasawwoq!) فلنذهب للتسوق!

Have you been shopping?

hal kunti tatasawwaqiin?

(hal konte tata sawwa qeen?) هل كنت تتسوقين؟

I like shopping.

'u<u>h</u>ibbut tasawwuq

(o<u>h</u>ebbot tasaw woq) أحب التسوق

I don't like shopping.

laa 'u<u>h</u>ibut tasawwuq

(laa o<u>h</u>ebbot tasaw woq) لا أحب التسوق

Is there a nearby shopping center?

hal yuujadu markaz tasawwuq qariib?

(hal yoojado markaz tasaw woq qareeb?)

هل يوجد مركز تسوق قريب؟

Have you been to Dubai for its Shopping Festival?
hal zurta mahrajaan dubayy lit tasawwuq?
(hal zorta mah ra jaan do bayy lettasaw woq?)
هل زرت مهرجان دبي للتسوق؟

84 **Buy** yashtarii *(yashtaree)* يشــتــري

I buy ... .
'anaa ashtarii *(anaa ashta ree)* أنا أشتري

I want to buy ... .
'uriidu 'an 'ashtarii… . *(oreedo an ash taree)*
أريــد أن أشــتري... .

I would like to buy it.
'awaddu 'an 'ashtariih *(awaddo an ashta reeh)*
أود أن أشتريه

I bought it.
ishtaraytuh *(eshta raytoh)* اشتريته

I am not going to buy it.
lan 'ashtariih *(lan ashta reeh)* لن أشتريه

Did you buy it?
halish taraytah? *(halesh taray tah?)* هل اشتريته؟

How much did you buy it for?

bika<u>mish</u> taraytah? *(be kame<u>sh</u> taray tah?)* بكم اشتريته؟

Who bought it?

mani<u>sh</u> taraah? *(mane<u>sh</u> taraah?)* من اشتراه؟

What do you want to buy?

maa<u>dh</u>aa turiid 'an ta<u>sh</u> tarii?

(maa<u>dh</u>aa tureed an ta<u>sh</u>ta ree?) ماذا تريد أن تشتري؟

Where did you buy that from?

min 'ayna<u>sh</u> taaraytah?

(men ayna<u>sh</u> taray tah?) من أين اشتريته؟

What did you buy?

maa<u>dhash</u> tarayt? *(maa <u>dhash</u> tarayt?)* ماذا اشتريت؟

85 Present & Souvenir

present: hadiyyah *(hadeyyah)* هــديــة
souvenir: ta<u>dh</u>kaar *(ta<u>dh</u> kaar)* تذكار

I bought you a present.

i<u>sh</u>taraytu laka hadiyyah *(e<u>sh</u> taray to laka hadeyyah)*

اشتريت لك هدية

Thanks for the present.

<u>sh</u>ukran `alal hadiyyah *(<u>sh</u>okan `alal hadeyyah)*

شكراً على الهدية

I hope you like my present.

'atamanna 'an tu`jibuka hadiyyatii *(ata mannaa an to` jeboka hadeyya tee)* أتمنى أن تعجبك هديتي

Is there a nearby gift shop?

hal hunaaka ma<u>h</u>al hadaayaa qariib? *(hal honaaka ma<u>h</u>al hadaayaa qareeb?)* هل هناك محل هدايا قريب؟

I bought you a souvenir.

i<u>sh</u>taraytu laka ta<u>dh</u>kaar *(e<u>sh</u> tarayto laka ta<u>dh</u> kaar)* اشتريت لك تذكار

Please accept my present.

'arjuu 'an taqbala hadiyyatii *(arjoo an taqbala ha deyyatee)* أرجو أن تقبل هديتى

I want to buy a present for my wife.

'uriidu 'an 'a<u>sh</u>tarii hadiyyatan li zawjatii *(oreedo an a<u>sh</u>ta reya hadeyyah le zaw jatee)* أريـد أن أشتـري هـديـة لـزوجـتي

86 Pay

yadfa` *(yadfa`)* يـدفـع

I will pay.

'anaa sa'adfa` *(anaa sa ad fa`)* أنا سأدفع

I paid.

'anaa dafa`t *(anaa da fa`t)* أنا دفعت

I didn't pay.

'anaa lam 'adfa` *(anaa lam ad fa`)* أنا لم أدفع

Who paid?

manil la<u>dh</u>ii dafa`?
(manel la <u>dh</u>ee da fa`?) من الذي دفع؟

Please don't pay.

'arjuuk laa tadfa` *(ar jook laa tad fa`)* أرجوك لا تدفع

I will pay cash.

sa'adfa`u naqdan *(sa ad fa `o naqdan)* سأدفع نقداً

Can I pay now?

hal 'asta<u>t</u>ii` 'an 'adfa`al 'aan? *(hal asta <u>t</u>ee` an ad fa `al aan?)* هل أستطيع أن أدفع الآن؟

Where can I pay?

'ayna yumkinu 'an 'adfa`?
(ayna yomkeno an ad fa`?) أين يمكن أن أدفع؟

I want to pay the bill.

'uriidu 'an 'adfa`al faatuurah law sama<u>h</u>t
(oreedo an ad fa`al faa too rah lao sama<u>h</u>t)
أريد أن أدفع الفاتورة لو سمحت

87 Price / Cost

price: si`r *(se`r)* سـعـر

cost: kulfah *(kol fah)* كلفة

What is the price please?

maa huwas si`r min fadlik?

(maa howas se`r men fad lek?)

مـا هـو الـسـعـر مـن فـضـلـك؟

How much does this cost?

kam yukallifu haadhaa?

(kam yokallefo haa dhaa?) كـم يـكـلـف هـذا؟

Is the price negotiable?

hali-si`r qaabil lit-tafaawud? *(hales se`r qaabel let tafaa wod?)* هـل الـسـعـر قـابـل لـلـتـفـاوض؟

Are the prices fixed here?

hali 'as`aar thaabitah hunaa?*(halel as `aar thaa betaton honaa?)* هـل الأسـعـار ثـابـتـة هـنـا؟

88 Rent yasta'jir (*yas ta' jer*) يسـتـأجـر

I want to rent a car.

'uriidu 'an 'asta'jira sayyaarah *(oreedo an as ta' jera sayyaarah)* أريـد أن أسـتـأجـر سـيـارة

What is the best place to rent a car?
maa afdalu makaanin listi'jaaris sayyaaraat?
(maa af dalo ma kaanen les te' jaares sayyaaraat?)
ما أفضل مكان لاستئجار السيارات؟

What's the nearest car rental office?
maa 'aqrabu maktab ta'jiir sayyaaraat?
(maa aq rabo maktab ta' jeer sayyaaraat?)
ما أقرب مكتب تأجير سيارات؟

Would renting a car be expensive here?
halis ti'jaaru sayyaarah muklif hunaa?
(hales te' jaaro sayyaarah moklef honaa?)
هل استئجار سيارة مكلف هنا؟

I want to rent a small apartment.
'uriidu 'an 'asta'jira shaqqatan saghiirah
(oreedo an as ta' jera shaqqa tan sa gheerah)
أريد أن أستأجر شقة صغيرة

What is the daily rent?
maa hiyal 'ujrah al yawmiyyah? *(maa heyal ojrah al yawmeyyah?)* ما هي الأجرة اليومية؟

What is the weekly rent?
maa hiyal 'ujrah al 'usbuu`iyyah?
(maa heyal ojrah al 'usbuu`iyyah?)
ما هي الأجرة الأسبوعية؟

I will pay the rent tomorrow.
sa'adfa`ul 'ujrah ghadan
(sa adfa `ol ojrah ghadan) سأدفع الأجرة غداً

I paid the rent.
laqad dafa`tul 'ujrah *(la qad da fa`tol ojrah)*
لقد دفعت الأجرة

89 Car sayyaarah *(sayyaarah)* سـيـارة

Do you have a car?
hal `indaka sayyaarah?
(hal `endaka sayyaarah?) هل عندك سيارة؟

I have a car.
`indii sayyaarah *(`endee sayyaarah)* عندي سيارة

I don't have a car.
laysa `indii sayyaarah
(laysa `endee sayyaarah) ليس عندي سيارة

Is this your car?
hal haadhihi sayyaaratuk?
(hal haa dhehe sayyaa ratok?) هل هذه سيارتك؟

I like your car.
sayyaaratuk tu`jibunii
(sayyaratok to` hebo nee) سيارتك تعجبني

I need a car.

'aḫtaaju 'ilaa sayyaarah *(aḫ taajo elaa sayyaarah)*

أحتاج إلى سيارة

Where is the car park?

'ayna maqqifus sayyaaraat?

(ayna maw qefos sayyaaraah?) أين موقف السيارات؟

I like 4 x 4 cars.

uḫibbi sayyaaraatad daf`ir rubaa`iyy

(oḫebbo sayyaa rated daf`err o baa `ee)

أحب سيارات الدفع الرباعيّ

I don't like driving manual cars.

laa uḫibbi qiyaadata as-sayyaraat dhaat an-naaqil al-yadawiyy *(laa oḫebbo qe yaa datas sayyaa raat dhaat annaaqel al yada wee)*

لا أحب قيادة السيارات ذات الناقل اليدوي

90 Mistake khaṯa' *(kha ṯa')* خطأ

Excuse me, I think I made a mistake.

al-ma`dhirah, aẕunni annanii 'akhṯa't

(al ma` dherah, aẕonno anna nee 'akh ṯa't)

المعذرة، أظن أنني أخطأت

Excuse me, I think you made a mistake.
al-ma`dhirah, azunnu ‘annaka akhta’t
(al ma` dherah, azonno annaka akh ta’t)
المعذرة، أظن أنك أخطأت

He made a mistake.
huwa akhta’ *(ho wa akhta’)* هو أخطأ

She made a mistake.
hiya ‘akhta’at *(heya akh ta’at)* هي أخطأت

There is no mistake.
laa yuujad khata’
(laa yoojado kha ta’) لا يوجد خطأ

There is a big mistake.
hunaaka khata’un kabiir *(honaaka kha ta on ka beer)*
هناك خطأ كبير

91 Lost daa`i *(daa e`)* ضائع

I am lost.
anaa daa’i` *(anaa daa e`)* أنا ضائع

We are lost.
nahnu daa’i`uun *(nahno daa e`oon)* نحن ضائعون

Are we lost?

hal nahno daa'i`uun? *(hal nahno daa e`oon?)*
هل نحن ضائعون؟

I was lost.

kuntu daa'i`an *(konto daa e`an)* كنت ضائعاً

I lost my bags.

'ada`tu haqaa'ibii *(ada`to ha qaa ebee)* أضعت حقائبي

I lost my money.

'ada`tu nuquudii *(ada`to noqoo dee)* أضعت نقودي

I lost my wallet.

'ada`tu mihfazatii *(ada`to meh fa zatee)*
أضعت محفظتي

I lost my way.

'ada`tu tariiqii *(ada`to ta ree qee)* أضعت طريقي

Excuse me, Sir / Madam. I am not from here and I lost my way. How can I get to ...?
al-ma`dhirah yaa sayyid /sayyidati, anaa lastu min hunaa wqad ada`tu tariiqii. kayfa asilu ilaa ...?
(al ma` dherah yaa sayyedee / sayyedatee, anaa lasto men honaa wa qad ada` to ta ree qee. kayfa aselo elaa ...?)
المعذرة يا سيدي / سيدتي، أنا لست من هنا وقد أضعت طريقي كيف أصل إلى ...؟

92 Sick mariid *(ma reed)* مريض

I am sick.
'anaa mariid *(anaa mareed)* أنا مريض

I am not sick.
'anaa lastu mariid *(anaa las to mareed)* أنا لست مريضا

I was sick.
kuntu mariid *(kon to mareed)* كنت مريضا

Are you sick?
hal 'anta mariid *(hal anta mareed?)* هل أنت مريض؟

Were you sick?
hal kunta mariid? *(hal konta mareed?)* هل كنت مريضا؟

The weather made me sick.
marid̲tu minal jaw *(ma red̲to menal jao)* مرضت من الجو

93 Pharmacy & Medicine

s̲aydaliyyah wa dawaa'
(s̲ay da leyyah wad a waa') صيدلية ودواء

Where is the pharmacy?
'ayna as̲ s̲aydaliyyah? *(aynas̲ s̲ay daleyyah?)*
أين الصيدلية؟

What time does the pharmacy open?
mataa taftah̲us̲ s̲aydaliyyah?
(mataa taf tahos̲ s̲ay daleyyah?)
متى تفتح الصيدلية؟

Is there a nearby pharmacy?
hal tuujadu s̲aydaliyyah qariibah?
(hal too jado saydaleyyah qa reebah?)
هل يوجد صيدلية قريبة؟

I want something for my cold.
uriidu dawaa'an lil-bard *(orreedo da waa an lel bard)*
أريد دواء للبرد

I want something for my cough.
uriidu dawaa'an lis-su`aal
(oreedo da waa an les so` daa`) أريد دواء للسعال

I want something for a headache.
'uriidu dawaa'an lis sudaa`
(oreedo da waa an les so daa`) أريد دواء للصداع

94 Doctor tabiib *(tabeeb)* طـبـيـب

I need to see a doctor.
'ahtaaju 'an 'araa tabiiban *(ah taajo an araa tabeeban)*
أحـتـاج أن أرى طـبـيـبـاً

Is there a doctor who speaks English?
hal yuujadu tabiibun yatakallamul inkliiziyyah?
(hal yoo jado tabeeb yata kallamol eng lee zeyyah?)
هـل يـوجـد طـبـيـبٌ يـتـكـلـم الإنـجـلـيـزيـة؟

Please call a doctor.
'arjuu 'an tattasila bit-tabiib
(ar joo an tatta sela bet tabeeb)
أرجـو أن تـتـصـل بـالـطـبـيـب

Call a doctor quickly!
ittasil bit-tabiib bisur`ah! *(etta sel bet tabeeb be sor `ah!)*
اتـصـل بـالـطـبـيـب بـسـرعـة

Have you called a doctor?
halit tasalta bittabiib ba`d?
(halet tasal ta bet tabeeb ba`d?)
هل اتصلت بالطبيب بعد؟

95 Dentist t̲abiib ‘asnaan *(t̲abeeb asnaan)*
طـبـيـب أسـنـان

Call a dentist please.

ittas̲il bi t̲abiibil ‘asnaan min fad̲lik

(ettasel be tabeebel asnaan men fad̲ lek)

اتصل بطبيب الأسنان من فضلك

I want to go to a dentist.

‘uriidu ‘an ad̲h̲ haba ‘ilaa t̲abiibi ‘asnaan

(oreedo an ad̲h̲ haba elaa t̲abee be asnaan)

أريد أن أذهب إلى طبيب أسنان

Is there a nearby dentist here?

hal yuujadu t̲abiibu ‘asnaan qariib hunaa?

(hal yoojado t̲abeebo asnaan qareeb honaa?)

هل يوجد طبيب أسنان قريب هنا؟

Going to a dentist is expensive here.

‘at̲ibba’ul ‘asnaan muklifuun hunaa *(at̲eb baa ol asnaan mok lefoon honaa)* أطباء الأسنان مكلفون هنا

Can you recommend a dentist?

hal tuus̲ii bi t̲abiibi ‘asnaan? *(hal too s̲ee bet̲a beebe asnaan?)* هـل تـوصـي بـطـبـيـب أسـنـان؟

96 Hospital

mustashfaa *(mos tash faa)* مـسـتـشـفـى

I need to go to the hospital.

'ahtaaju 'an 'adh haba 'ilal mustashfaa *(ah taajo an adh haba elal mos tash faa)* أحتاج أن أذهب إلى المستشفى

We took him / her to the hospital.

'akhadhnaa(hu) /(haa) 'ilal mustashfaa *(akhadh naa(ho) /(haa) elal mos tash faa)* أخذناه إلى المستشفى

Let's go to another hospital!

fal nadh hab 'ilaa mustashfan 'aakhar!

(fal nadh hab elaa mos tash fan aa khar!)

فلنذهب إلى مستشفى آخر!

Is there a children's hospital here?

hal yuujadu mustashfaa 'atfaal?

(hal yoojado mos tash faa at faal?)

هل يوجد مستشفى أطفال؟

I am at the hospital.

'anaa bil mustashfaa *(anaa bel mos tash faa)*

أنا بالمستشفى

Is there a nearby hospital?
hal yuujadu musta<u>sh</u>fan qariibun min hunaa?
(hal yoo jado mos ta<u>sh</u>fan qareeb men honaa?)
هــل يــوجــد مــســتــشــفى قــريــب؟

Take me to the hospital.
<u>kh</u>u<u>dh</u>nii' ilal musta<u>sh</u>faa *(<u>kh</u>o<u>dh</u> nee elal mos ta<u>sh</u> faa)*
خذنــي إلــى الــمــســتــشــفى

97 Ambulance

sayyaarat 'is`aaf *(sayyaarat es `aaf)*
سيارة إســعــاف

Please call an ambulance.
itta<u>s</u>il bisayyaratil 'is`aaf rajaa'an
(etta sel be sayya ratel es`aaf ra jaa an)
اتــصــل بــسيارة الإســعــاف رجــاءً

It's urgent, we need an ambulance.
'innahaa <u>h</u>aalatun <u>t</u>aari'ah, nahtaaju 'ilaa sayyarati 'is`aaf *(enna <u>h</u>aa haa laton <u>t</u>aa re ah, nah taajo elaa sayyarat es `aaf)*
إنــهــا حــالــة طــارئــة، نحتاج إلى سيارة إسعاف

Take him / her to the hospital.
<u>kh</u>u<u>dh</u> (hu) / (<u>h</u>aa) 'ilal-musta<u>sh</u>faa
(<u>kh</u>o<u>dh</u> (ho) / (<u>h</u>aa) elal mos ta<u>sh</u> faa)
خــذ(هــا) / (ه) إلــى الــمــســتــشــفــى

She was hit by a car. Please call an ambulance!
sadamathaa sayyaarah, ittasil bi sayyaratil ‘is`aaf
(sa damat haa sayyaarah, etta sel be sayya ratel ‘es `aaf)
صدمتها سيارة، اتصل بسيارة الإسعاف

What is the number to call the ambulance?
maa raqmul sayyaratil ‘is`aaf? *(maa raq mo sayya ratel es `aaf?)* ما رقم سيارة الإسعاف؟

Have you called an ambulance yet?
halit tasalta bisayyaratil ‘is`aaf ba`d?
(halet tasalta be sayya ratel es `aaf ba`d?)
هل اتصلت بسيارة الإسعاف بعد؟

98 Police shurtah *(shor tah)* شرطة

Call the police!
ittasil bish shurtah *(et tasel besh short ah)*
اتصل بالشرطة

I have to call the police.
`alayya ‘an ‘attasila bish shurtah
(`alayya an atta sela besh shortah)
عليّ أن أتصل بالشرطة

Did you call the police?
halit tasalta bish shurtah? *(hal etta salta besh short ah?)*
هل اتصلت بالشرطة؟

What is the number for the police?
maa raqmu<u>sh</u> <u>sh</u>ur<u>t</u>ah?
(maa raq mo<u>sh</u> <u>sh</u>or<u>t</u>ah?) ما رقم الشرطة؟

Take me to the nearest police station, please.
<u>kh</u>u<u>dh</u>nii ‘ilaa ‘aqrabi markazi <u>sh</u>ur<u>t</u>ah
(<u>kh</u>o<u>dh</u> nee elaa aqrabe marka ze <u>sh</u>ort ah)
خذني إلى أقرب مركز شرطة

99 Embassy safaarah *(sa faa rah)* سـفـارة

I want to go to the … .
‘uriidu ‘an ‘a<u>dh</u>-haba ‘ilaa… .
(oree do an a<u>dh</u> haba elaa… .)
أريـد أن أذهـب إلـى … .

Australian embassy
as-safaarah al-usturaaliyyah
(assa faarah al osto raaleyyah)
الـسـفـارةالأسـتـرالـيـة

American embassy
assafaarh al-amriikiyyah
(assa faarah al amreekeyyah) الـسـفارة الأمـريـكـيـة

British embassy
assafaarah al-brii<u>t</u>aaniyyah *(assa faarah al bree <u>t</u>aaneyyah)* الـسـفـارةالـبـريـطـانـيـة

French embassy

assafaarah al-faransiyyah *(assa faarah al faran seyyah)*
الـسـفـارة الـفـرنـسـيـة

Italian embassy

assafaarah al-'iitaaliyyah *(assa faa rah al eetaa leyyah)*
الـسـفـارة الإيـطـالـيـة

Portuguese embassy

assafaarah al-burtughaaliyyah
(assa faarah al borto ghaa leyyah)
الـسـفـارة الـبـرتـغـالـيـة

German embassy

assafaarah al-almaaniyyah
(assa faarah al alma neyyah) الـسـفـارة الألـمـانـيـة

Where is the Australian embassy?

'aynas safaaratul 'usturaaliyyah? *(aynas safaa ratol osto raaleyyah?)* أين السفارة الأسترالية؟

Is there an Australian embassy here?

hal yuujadu safaaratun 'usturaaliyyah hunaa?
(hal yoo jado safaa raton osto raa leyyah honaa?)
هل يوجد سفارة أسترالية هنا؟

I want to meet the ambassador.
'uriidu 'an 'uqaabilas safiir
(oree do an oqaa belas safer)
أريــد أن أقــابــل الــســفــيــر

What is the number of the ... embassy?
maa raqamus safaaratil....?
(maa raqmos safaa ratel ....?)
مــا رقــم الــســفــارة الــ....؟

100 Numbers al-'arqaam *(al-'arqaam)* الأرقــام

0	sifr *(sefr)*	٠
1	waahid *(waa hed)*	١
2	ithnaan *(eth naan)*	٢
3	thalaathah *(thalaa thah)*	٣
4	arba`ah *(arba`ah)*	٤
5	khamsah *(kham sah)*	٥
6	sittah *(settah)*	٦
7	sab`ah *(sab`ah)*	٧
8	thamaaniyah *(thamaa neyah)*	٨
9	tis`ah *(tes `ah)*	٩
10	`asharah *(`ash rah)*	١٠
11	ahada`ashar *(ahada `ashar)*	١١
12	ithnaa `ashar *(ethnaa `ashar)*	١٢
13	thalaathata `ashar *(thalaa thata `ashar)*	١٣
14	arba`ata `ashar *(arba`ata `ashar)*	١٤
15	khamsata `ashar *(khamsata `ashar)*	١٥

16 sittata `ashar *(settata `ashar)* ١٦

17 sab`ata `ashar *(sab`ata `ashar)* ١٧

18 thamaaniyata `ashar
(thamaaneyata `ashar) ١٨

19 tis`ata `ashar *(tes`ata `ashar)* ١٩

20 `ishruun *(`esh roon)* ٢٠

21 waahid wa`ishruun
(waahed wa `eshroon) ٢١

22 ithnaan wa`ishruun
(ethnaan wa eshroon) ٢٢

23 thalaathah wa`ishruun
(thalaathah wa `eshroon) ٢٣

24 arba`ah wa`ishruun
(arba`ah wa `eshroon) ٢٤

25 khamsah wa`ishruun
(khamsah wa `eshroon) ٢٥

26 sittah wa`ishruun
(settah wa `eshroon) ٢٦

27 sab`ah wa`ishruun
(sab`ah wa `eshroon) ٢٧

28 thamaaniyah wa`ishruun
(thamaaneya wa `eshroon) ٢٨

29 tis`ah wa`ishruun
(tes`ah wa `eshroon) ٢٩

30 thalaathuun *(thalaa thoon)* ٣٠

40 arba`uun *(arba`oon)* ٤٠

50 khamsuun *(khamsoon)* ٥٠

60 sittuun *(settoon)* ٦٠

70	sab`uun *(sab`oon)*	٧٠
80	thamaanuun *(thamaanoon)*	٨٠
90	tis`uun *(tes`oon)*	٩٠
100	mi'ah *(me ah)*	١٠٠
101	mi'ah wawaahid *(me ah wa waahed)*	١٠١
102	mi'ah wa'ithnaan *(me ah wa ethnaan)*	١٠٢
103	mi'ah wathalaathah *(me ah wa thalaathah)*	١٠٣
104	mi'ah wa'arba`ah *(me ah wa arba`ah)*	١٠٤
105	mi'ah wakhamsah *(me ah wa khamsah)*	١٠٥
106	mi'ah wasittah *(me ah wa settah)*	١٠٦
107	mi'ah wasab`ah *(me ah wa sab`ah)*	١٠٧
108	mi'ah wathamaaniyah *(me ah wa tha maaneyah)*	١٠٨
109	mi'ah watis`ah *(me ah wa tes `ah)*	١٠٩
110	mi'ah wa`asharah *(me ah wa `ash rah)*	١١٠
120	mi'ah wa`ishruun *(me ah wa `eshroon)*	١٢٠
130	mi'ah wathalaathuun *(me ah wa thalaathoon)*	١٣٠
140	mi'ah wa'arba`uun *(me ah wa arba`oon)*	١٤٠
150	mi'ah wakhamsiin *(me ah wa khamsoon)*	١٥٠
160	mi'ah wasittuun *(me ah wa settoon)*	١٦٠
170	mi'ah wasab`uun *(me ah wa sab`oon)*	١٧٠
180	mi'ah wathamaanuun *(me ah wa thamaanoon)*	١٨٠

190	mi'ah watis`uun *(me ah wa tes`oon)*	١٩٠
200	mi'ataan *(me ataan)*	٢٠٠
201	mi'ataan wawaahid *(me ataan wa waahed)*	٢٠١
300	thalaathumi'ah *(thalaatho me ah)*	٣٠٠
400	arba`u mi'ah *(arba`o me ah)*	٤٠٠
500	khamsu mi'ah *(khamso me ah)*	٥٠٠
600	sittu mi'ah *(setto me ah)*	٦٠٠
700	sab`u mi'ah *(sab`o me ah)*	٧٠٠
800	thamaanu mi'ah *(tha maano me ah)*	٨٠٠
900	tis`u mi'ah *(tes`o me ah)*	٩٠٠
1,000	alf *(alf)*	١٠٠٠
1,500	alf wakhamsu mi'ah *(alf wa khamso me ah)*	١٥٠٠
2,000	alfaan *(alfaan)*	٢٠٠٠
3,000	thalaathat 'aalaaf *(thalaathat aa laaf)*	٣٠٠٠
4,000	arba`at 'aalaaf *(arba`at aa laaf)*	٤٠٠٠
5,000	khamsat 'aalaaf *(khamsat aa laaf)*	٥٠٠٠
6,000	sittat 'aalaaf *(settat aa laaf)*	٦٠٠٠
7,000	sab`at 'aalaaf *(sab`at aa laaf)*	٧٠٠٠
8,000	thamaaniyah 'aalaaf *(thamaa neyat aa laaf)*	٨٠٠٠
9,000	tis`at 'aalaaf *(tes `at aa laaf)*	٩٠٠٠
10,000	`ashrat 'aalaaf *(`asharat aa laaf)*	١٠٠٠٠
11,000	ahada `ashara alf *(ahada `ashara alf)*	١١٠٠٠

12,000	ithnaa `ashara alf *(ethnaa `ashara alf)*	١٢٠٠٠
17,000	sab`ata `ashara alf *(sab`ata `ashara alf)*	١٧٠٠٠
100,000	mi'at alf *(me at alf)*	١٠٠٠٠٠
250,000	rub` milyuun *(rob` melyoon)*	٢٥٠٠٠٠
500,000	nisf milyuun *(nesf melyoon)*	٥٠٠٠٠٠
1,000,000	milyuun *(lelyoon)*	١٠٠٠٠٠٠

PART 2

Additional Vocabulary

Arab Countries and Some Major Cities

ad-duwal al-`arabiyyah wa ba`d al-mudun ar-ra'i-isiyyah *(addo wal al `ara beyyah wa ba`do almod-on arra 'eeseyyah)*
الدول العربية وبعض المدن الرئيسية

- **Algeria** al-jazaa'ir *(al jazaa er)* الجزائر

Algiers	al-jazaa`ir *(al jazaa `er)*	الجزائر
Oran	wahraan *(wahraan)*	وهران
Tlemcen	tilmasaan *(tel masaan)*	تلمسان
Constantine	qasantiina *(qasan teena)*	قسنطينة
Annaba	`annaabah *(`annaabah)*	عنابة

- **Bahrain** al-bahrayn *(albah rein)* البحرين

Manamah	al-manaamah *(al-manaamah)*	المنامة
Almuharraq	al-muharraq *(al moharraq)*	المحرق

Comoros juzur al-qumur *(jozor alqo mor)* القمر

Moroni murunii *(moo roo nee)* موروني

- **Djibouti** jiibuutii *(jee boo tee)* جيبوتي

Djibouti jiibuutii *(jee boo tee)* جيبوتي

- **Egypt** misr *(mesr)* مصر

Cairo al-qaahirah *(alqaa herah)* القاهرة

Alexandra al-iskandariyyah *(al eskan dareyyah)* الإسكندرية

Ismaeliyya al-isma`iiliyyah *(ales maa `ee leyyah)* الإسماعيلية

Aswan aswaan *(aswaan)* أسوان

El-Suwies as-suwais *(asso weis)* السويس

Dumyat dimyaat *(dem yaat)* دمياط

- **Emirates** al-imaaraat *(alemaa raat)* الإمارات

Abu Dhabi abuu zabii *(aboo zabee)* أبو ظبي

Dubai dubayy *(do bayy)* دبي

Sharja ash-shaariqah *(ash shaa re qah)* الشارقة

El-Ein al-`iyn *(al `ein)* العين

Ajman `ajmaan *(`ajmaan)* عجمان

El-Fujeirah al-fujairah *(al-fujairah)* الفجيرة

Ras El-Kheimah	ra's al-khaimah *(raasel khei mah)*	أس الخيمة

- **Iraq** al-`iraaq *(al `eraaq)* العراق

Baghdad	baghdaad *(baghdaad)*	بغداد
Mousel	al-muusil *(al moo sel)*	الموصل
Basrah	al-basrah *(al bas rah)*	البصرة
Nassiriyyah	an-naasiriyyah *(anna sereyyah)*	الناصرية
Najaf	an-najaf *(an-najaf)*	نجف
Kirkuk	karkuuk *(kar kook)*	كركوك
Dhuk	duhuk *(do hook)*	دهوك
Arbil	arbiil *(ar beel)*	أربيل

- **Jordan** al-urdun *(al or don)* الأردن

Amman	`ammaan *(`ammaan)*	عمّان
Irbid	irbid *(er bed)*	إربد
Zerka	az-zarqaa' *(az-zarqaa')*	الزرقاء
Jerash	jarash *(jarash)*	جرش
Karak	al-karak *(al-karak)*	الكرك
Tafilah	at-tafiilah *(atta fee lah)*	الطفيلة
Aqaba	al-`aqabah *(al-`aqabah)*	العقبة
Ajloun	`ajluun *(`aj loon)*	عجلون

- **Kuwait** al-kuwayt *(al kowayyt)* الكويت

Kuwait	al-kuwayt *(al ko wayyt)*	الكويت

- **Lebanon** Lubnaan *(lob naan)* لبنان

Beirut	bayruut *(bayy root)*	بيروت
Tripoli	talaablus *(ta raab los)*	طرابلس
Sidon	saydaa *(saydaa)*	صيدا
Tyre	suur *(soor)*	صور
Baalbeck	b`albak *(b`albak)*	بعلبك

- **Libya** liibyaa ليبيا

Tripoli	taraablus *(ta raab los)*	طرابلس
Banghazi	banghaazii *(ban ghaa zee)*	بنغازي
Tubruq	tubruq *(tob roq)*	طبرق

- **Morocco** al-maghrib *(al magh reb)* المغرب

Rabat	ar-rabaat *(arra baat)*	الرباط
Casablanca	ad-daar al-baydaa' *(ad-daar al-baydaa')*	الدار البيضاء
Marrakech	maraakish *(maraa kesh)*	مراكش
Fes	faas *(faas)*	فاس
Meknas	maknaas *(maknaas)*	مكناس
Aghadir	aghaadiir *(aghaa deer)*	أغادير

- **Mauritania** muriitaanyaa *(mo ree taa nyaa)* موريتانيا

Nouakchott	nawaakshut *(na waak shot)*	نواكشوط
Chanqit	shanqiit *(shan qeet)*	شنقيط

- **Oman** `umaan *(`o maan)* عُمان

Muscat masqat *(mas qat)* مسقط
Salalah salaalah *(salaalah)* جبال صلالة
Sour suur *(soor)* صور

- **Palestine** falastiin *(falas teen)* فلسطين

Jerusalem al-quds *(al qods)* القدس
Ramallah raamallah *(raamallah)* رام الله
Bethlehem bait-lahim *(beit la hem)* بيت لحم
Nablus naablis *(naab les)* نابلس
Gaza ghazzah *(ghazzah)* غزّة
Hebron al-khaliil *(alkha leel)* الخليل
Jenin jiniin (*je neen*) جنين
Toulkarem tuulkarim (*tool karem*) طولكرم
Jericho ‘ariihaa *(aree haa)* أريحا

- **Qatar** qatar *(qatar)* قطر

Doha ad-dawhah *(addao hah)* الدوحة

- Saudi Arabia as-su`uudiyyah *(asso `oo deyyah)* السعودية

Riyadh ar-riyaad *(ar-riyaad)* الرياض
Mecca makkah *(makkah)* مكة
Medina al-madiinah *(al madee mah)* المدينة
Jeddah jaddah *(jaddah)* جدة
Dammam ad-dammaam *(ad-dammaam)* الدمام
Abha abhaa *(abhaa)* أبها

Tabouk tabuuk *(taboo k)* تبوك

- **Somalia** as-suumaal *(assoo maal)* الصومال

Magadishu maqadiishu *(maqa dee sho)* مقديشو
Berbera barbarah *(barbarah)* بربرة

- **Sudan** as-suudaan *(assoo daan)* السودان

Khartum al-khurtuum *(al khor toom)* الخرطوم
Omdurman um durmaan *(om dar maan)* أم درمان
Port Sudan bur suudaan *(bor soodaan)* بور سودان
Kassala kasala *(kasala)* كسلا
Juba juubaa *(joo baa)* جوبا

- **Syria** suuryaa *(soor yaa)* سوريا

Damascus dimashq *(de mashq)* دمشق
Alippo halab *(halab)* حلب
Latakia al-laadhiqiyyah *(allaa dhe qeyyah)* اللاذقية
Homs hims *(hems)* حمص
Palmyra tadmur *(tad mor)* تدمر
Al-Hasakeh al-hasakih *(al hasa ke)* الحسكة
Tartous tartuus *(tar toos)* طرطوس
Banyas baanyaas *(baanyaas)* بانياس

• **Tunisia** tuunis *(too nes)* تــونــس

Tunis	tuunis *(too nes)*	تــونــس
Bizerte	binzart *(ben zart)*	بــنــزرت
Sfax	<u>s</u>afaaqis *(<u>s</u>afaa qes)*	صــفــاقــس
Sousse	suusa *(soo sah)*	ســوســة
Gabes	qaabis *(gaa bes)*	قــابــس
Monastir	al-munastiir *(al monas teer)*	الــمــنــســتــيــر
Kairouan	al-qayrawaan *(al qayy rawaan)*	الــقــيــروان
Jerba	jirbah *(jerba)*	جــربــة
Tabarka	<u>t</u>abarqa *(<u>t</u>abarqa)*	طــبــرقــة

• **Yemen** al-yaman *(al-yaman)* الــيــمــن

Sana'a	san`aa' *(san`aa')*	صــنــعــاء
Aden	`adan *(`adan)*	عــدن
Ta'az	ta'z *(ta'z)*	تــعــز
Al Hudaydah	al-<u>h</u>udaydah *(al-<u>h</u>udaydah)*	الــحــديــدة

Famous Landmarks in the Arab World

ma`aalim <u>sh</u>ahiirah fii al-`aalam al-`arabiyy *(ma`aa lem <u>sh</u>ahee rah fel `aalamel `ara bee)*

مــعالــم شــهــيرة فــي الــعــالــم الــعــربــي

Muslim holy sites

mawaaqi` muqaddasah islaamiyyah *(mawaa qe` moqadda sah eslaa meyyah)* مــواقــع مــقــدســة إسلامــيــة

Ka`aba (Mecca – Saudi Arabia) al-ka`bah *(al-ka`bah)*
الكعبة

Prophet's Mosque (Medinah–Saudi Arabia)
al-masjid an-nabawiyy *(almas jedon naba wee)*
المسجد النبوي

Dome of the Rock & Al-Aqsa Mosque (Jerusalem–Palestine)
qubbat as-sakhrah wal-masjid al-aqsaa *(qobba tos sakhrah wal mas jedol aqsaa)*
قبة الصخرة والمسجد الأقصى

Christian holy sites
mawaaqi` muqaddasah masiihiyyah *(mawaa qe` moqad dasah masee heyyah)*
مواقع مقدسة مسيحية

Church Of Nativity *(Bethlehem–Palestine)*
kaniisat al-mahd *(kanee satol mahd)*
كنيسة المهد

Church Of The Holy Sepulchre *(Jerusalem–Palestine)*
kaniisat al-qiyaamah *(kanee satol qeyaa mah)*
كنيسة القيامة

Tourist Destinations

wujhaat siyaahiyyah *(woj haat seyaa heyyah)*
وجهات سياحية

- **Egypt** misr *(mesr)* مصر

  Cairo al-qaahirah *(alqaa herah)* القاهرة

  Giza Pyramids ahraamaat al-jiizah *(ahraa maatel jeezah)*
  أهرامات الجيزة

  Mohamed Ali Mosque jaami` muhammad `alii
  (jaa me` mohammad `alee) جامع محمد علي

  Al-Azhar al-azhar *(al-azhar)* الازهر

  Egyptian Museum
  al-muthaf al-misriyy *(almot hafol masree)*
  المتحف المصري

  Museum of Islamic Arts
  muthaf al-funuun al-islaamiyyah *(mot hafol fonoonel eslaa meyyah)* متحف الفنون الإسلامية

  Coptic Museum al-muthaf al-qibtiyy
  (almot hafol qebtee) المتحف القبطى

- **Luxor** al-uqsur *(al oqsor)* الأقصر

  Temple of Luxor ma`bad al-uqsur *(ma`badol oqsor)*
  معبد الأقصر

  Temple of Karnak ma`bad al-karnak *(ma`bad al-karnak)*
  معبد الكرنك

  Valley of the Kings
  waadii al-muluuk *(waadel molook)* وادي الملوك

- **Alexandria** al'iskandariyyah *(aleskan da reyya)*
  الإسكندرية

  Almontazah Palace qasr al-muntazah *(qas rel monta zah)*
  صر المنتزه

- **Iraq** al-`iraaq *(al `eraaq)* العراق

  Baghdad baghdaad *(bagh daad)* بغداد

  Baghdad Museum
  muthaf baghdaad *(mot haf bagh daad)*
  متحف بغداد

  Khan Murjan
  khan murjaan *(khaan mor jaan)* خان مرجان

Abbasid Palace
qasr al-`abbaasiyyiin *(qa<u>s</u>r al`abbaa seyyeen)*
قصر العباسيين

Mustansiriyya School
madrasat al-mustan<u>s</u>iriyyah *(mad rasatol mostan <u>s</u>ereyyah)*
مدرسة المستنصرية

Iraqi Museum
al-mut<u>h</u>af al-`iraaqiyy *(almot <u>h</u>afol `era qee)*
المتحف العراقي

- **Lebanon** lubnaan *(lob naan)* لبنان

Baalbeck Roman City
madiinat b`albak ar-rumaaniyyah
(madee nat b`al bakerroo maa neyyah)
مدينة بعلبك الرومانية

Aanjar `anjar *(`anjar)* عنجر

- **Jordan** al-urdun *(al or don)* الأردن

Jerash jara<u>sh</u> *(jara<u>sh</u>)* جرش

Temple of Artemis
ma`bad artimiis *(ma`bad arte mees)*
معبد أرتيميس

Roman Baths
al-hammaamaat ar-rumaaniyyah
(al hammaa maaterroo maa neyyah)
الحمامات الرومانية

Christian cathedral
al-kaatidraa'iyyah al-masiihiyyah
(alkaa ted raa eyyah al masee heyyah)
الكاتدرائية المسيحية

Street of Columns
shaari` al-a`midah *(shaa re `ol a`medah)*
شارع الأعمدة

- **Madaba** maadabaa *(maadabaa)* مادبا

Mosaic al-fusayfisaa' *(alfo sayfe saa')*
الفسيفساء

Petra Al-batraa' *(Al-batraa')* البتراء

The Treasury al-khaznah *(al-khaznah)* الخزنة

Mountain of Rum jabal ramm *(jabal ramm)* جبل رم

- **Syria** suuryaa *(soor yaa)* سوريا

Damascus dimashq *(de mashq)* دمشق

Omayyad Mosque
al-jaami` al-umawiyy *(aljaa me`ol ama wee)*
الجامع الأموي

Azem Palace qa<u>s</u>r al-`a<u>z</u>m *(qa<u>s</u>r al-`a<u>z</u>m)*
قصر العظم

Hamidiyyeh Souk
suuq al-<u>h</u>amiidiyyah *(soo qel <u>h</u>amee deyyah)*
سوق الحميدية

Mt Kassioun jabal qaasyuun *(jabal qaas yoon)*
جبل قاسيون

Palmyra tadmur *(tad mor)* تدمر

Temple of Bell
ma`bad al-jaras *(ma` badel jaras)* معبد الجرس

Aleppo <u>h</u>alab *(<u>h</u>alab)* حلب

Khan el Jomruk
<u>kh</u>aan al-jumruk *(<u>kh</u>aanel jom rok)* خان الجمرك

Atroush Mosque
jaami` al-`a<u>t</u>ruu<u>sh</u> *(jaa me`ol `a<u>t</u> roo<u>sh</u>)*
جامع العطروش

School of Paradise
madrasat al-jannah *(mad rasa tol jannah)*
مـدرسـة الـجـنـة

Bab Antakia
baab antaakyaa *(baab antaakyaa)* بـاب أنـطـاكـيـا

Bab El Makam
baab al-maqaam *(baab al-maqaam)* بـاب الـمـقـام

Hama hamaah *(hamaah)* حـمـاة

Nawers of Hama nawaa`iir hamaah
(nawaa `eer hamaah) نـواعـيـر حـمـاة

- **Oman** `umaan *(`umaan)* عُـمـان

Western Hajar Mountains
jibaal al-hajar al-gharbiyy *(jaba lel haja rel ghar bee)*
جـبـل الـحـجـر الـغـربـي

Salalah Mountains
jibaal salaalah *(jibaal salaalah)* جـبـال صـلالـة

Jabal Akhdar
al-jabal al-akhdar *(al-jabal al-akhdar)*
الـجـبـل الأخـضـر

- **Yemen** al-yaman *(al-yaman)* اليمن

  Sana san`aa' *(san`aa')* صنعاء

  Rock House bait as-sakhrah *(baytos sakhrah)* بيت الصخرة

  The Old City Wall
  jidaar al-madiinah al-qadiimah *(jedaa rol made nah al qadee mah)* المدينة القديمة

  Palace of Ghamdan
  qasr ghamadaan *(qasr ghamadaan)* قصر غمدان

- **Tunis** tuunis *(toones)* تونس

  El Zaytuna Mosque
  jaami` az-zaytuunah *(jaame`oz zaytoonah)* الزيتونة

  Carthage Ruins
  al-mantiqah al-'athariyyah bi qartaaj
  (alman teqah al atha reyyah be qar taaj)
  المَنْطِقة الأثرية بقرطاج

  Bardo Museum
  muthaf baardu *(mot haf baardo)* متحف باردو

Lake of Tunis
buhayrat tuunis *(bohayrat toones)*
بحيرة تونس

Kairouan
madiinat al-qayrawaan *(madee natol qayyra waan)*
مدينة القيروان

Uqbah Ben Nafi' Mosque
jaami` `uqbah bin naafi` *(jaame` `oqbah ben naa fe`)*
جامع عقبة بن نافع

El Jem Roman Amphitheater
al-masrah ar-rumaaniyy bil-jim *(almasrah arroo maanee bel jem)* المسرح الروماني بالجم

Douz Oasis
waahat duuz *(waa hat dooz)* واحة دوز

Matmata ***(Berber town)***
mantiqat matmaatah *(man teqat mat maa tah)*
منطقة مطماطة

Hammamet
al-hammaamaat *(al-hammaamaat)* الحمامات

Jerba Island
jaziirat jirba *(jazeerat jarbaa)* جزيرة جربا

- **Morocco** al-ma<u>gh</u>rib *(al-maghrib)* الـــمـــغـــرب

Casablanca
ad-daar al-bay<u>d</u>aa' *(adda rol baydaa)*
الـــدار الـــبـــيـــضـــاء

Hassan II Mosque
jaami` al-<u>h</u>asan a<u>th</u>-<u>th</u>aanii *(jaa me` al-hasaneth thaanee)*
جـــامـــع الـــحـــســـن الـــثـــانـــي

Old Medina
al-madiinah al-qadiimah *(alma deenah alqa deemah)*
الـــمـــديـــنـــة الـــقـــديـــمـــة

City Hall
saa<u>h</u>at al-madiinah *(saahatol madee nah)*
ســـاحـــة الـــمـــديـــنـــة

- **Fes** faas *(faas)* فـــاس

Gates of Fes
bawwaabaat faas *(bawwaabaat faas)* بـــوابـــات فـــاس

Attarin School
madrasat al-`a<u>tt</u>aariin *(madra satol `attaa reen)*
مـــدرســـة الـــعـــطـــاريـــن

Kairaouine Mosque
jaami` al-qarawwiyyiin *(jaa me`ol qara weyyeen)*
جـامع الـقـرويـيـن

- **Marrakech** marraaki<u>sh</u> *(maraa ke<u>sh</u>)* مـراكـش

Bahia Palace
qa<u>s</u>r baahya *(qa<u>s</u>r baahya)* قـصـر بـاهـية

Ali Ben Youssef School
madrasat `alii bin yuusif *(mad rasat `alee ben yoo sef)*
مـدرسـة عـلي بـن يـوسـف

Koutobia Mosque and Minaret
masjid wa manaarat al-qu<u>t</u>biyyah *(masjed wa manaa ratel qo<u>t</u> beyyah)* مـسـجـد ومـنـارة الـقـطـبـيـة

- **Rabat** ar-rabaat *(ar-rabaat)* الـربـاط

Mausoleum of Mohammad V
<u>d</u>arii<u>h</u> mu<u>h</u>ammad al-<u>kh</u>aamis *(<u>d</u>a ree<u>h</u> mo hammadel <u>kh</u>aa mes)* ضـريـح مـحـمـد الـخـامـس

Royal Palace of Rabat
qa<u>s</u>r ar-rabaa<u>t</u> al-malakiyy *(q<u>a</u>s rorre baa<u>t</u>el mala kee)*
قـصـر الـربـاط الـمـلـكـي

Islamic Expressions

ta`aabiir islaamiyyah *(ta`aa beer eslaa meyyah)*
تعابير إسلامية

There are different Islamic formulaic terms and common expressions used widely on different occasions. Here is a sample of some of the most frequent amongst them.

"Peace be upon you"—the greeting of the Muslim
as-salaamu `alaykum *(assa laamo `alayy kom)*
السلام عليكم

The reply **is "and peace be upon you"**
wa`alaykumus salaam *(wa `alayy komos salaam)*
وعليكم السلام

The fuller version reads:
"Peace be upon you and the blessings and mercy of Allah"
as-salaamu `alaykum wa ra<u>h</u>matul laahi wa barakaatuh
(assa laamo `alayy kom wara<u>h</u> matol laahe wa bara kaa toh)
السلام عليكم ورحمة الله وبركاته

The reply is:
"And upon you be the peace and Allah's mercy and blessings"
wa `alaykum as-salaam warahmatu allaahi wa barakaatuh *(wa `alayyko mos salaam wa rah matol laahe wa bara kaa toh)* وعليكم السلام ورحمة الله وبركاته

Although this expression means **"praises belong to Allah"** or **"Thanks to God,"** it is used widely as a response to **"How are you?,"** as Muslims tend to thank God to express their wellbeings.
al-hamdu lillaah *(al hamdo lel laah)* الحمد لله

Usually said when referring to a situation in the future e.g. **"inshAllah, I will go to the grocery shop tomorrow,"** etc, and it means **"If Allah wills."**

inshaa'Allaah *(enshaa allaah)* إن شاء الله

Used when someone returns from a long trip (ie overseas), or survives a sickness or an accident and it means **"Thanks God for your safety"**
al-hamdulillaah `alas salaamah *(alham dolel laahe `alas salaam ah)* الحمد لله على السلامة

Used at the end of prayers meaning **"Please accept."**
'aamiin *(aa meen)* آمين

"Allah is greater." Also called the *takbiir* and used to express astonishment or excitement
Allaahu akbar *(allaho akbar)* الـلـه أكـبـر

"Allah knows best." This expression is used as in "I don't know."
Allaahu a`lam *(allaho a` lam)* الـلـه أعـلـم

"I ask forgiveness from Allah."
'astaghrirul laah *(astagh ferol laah)* أسـتـغـفـر الـلـه

"I seek protection in Allah from the accursed satan."
'a`uudhu billaahi minash-shaytaanir rajiim *(a`oo dho bel-laahe menash shaytaaner rajeem)*
أعـوذ بـالـلـه مـن الـشـيـطـان الـرجـيـم

Also known as *basmalah* and meaning **"In the name of Allah, the all Merciful, the most Compassionate."** This expression is widely used to begin a speech, letter, contract and/or before eating.

bismillahir rahmaanir rahiim *(besmel laaher rahmaa nerra heem)* بـسـم الـلـه الـرحـمـن الـرحـيـم

Used after mentioning the name of Allah to mean **"Mighty and Majestic is He"**
`azza wa jall *(`azza wa jall)* عـز وجـلّ

"May the blessings of Allah be upon you"—used when a Muslim wants to thank another person to express his /her thanks, appreciation and gratitude.
baarakal laahu fiik *(baa rakal laaho feek)*
بـارك الـلـه فـيـك

"In Allah's protection"—used to bide farewell to someone.
fii 'amaanil laah *(fee amaa nellaah)* فـي أمـان الـلـه

"There is no power nor strength save (except) by Allah"—used when someone is struck with calamity, or is taken over by a situation beyond his/her control.
laa <u>h</u>awla walla quwwata illaa billaah *(laa <u>h</u>awla walaa qowwata ellaa bellaah)* لا حـول ولا قـوة إلا بـالـلـه

Kuranic expression meaning **"We are from Allah and to Him we shall return."** It is usually said upon hearing of the death of an individual.
innaa lillaahi wa innaa ilayhi raaji`uun *(ennaa lellaah wa enna elayyhe raa je`oon)* إنـا لـلـه وإنـا إلـيـه راجـعـون

"May Allah's mercy be upon him/her."
ra<u>h</u>imahu /ra<u>h</u>imahaa *(fem)* Allaah *(ra <u>h</u>em hollaah / ra <u>h</u>ema hallaah* (fem)*)* رحـمـه/ رحـمـهـا الـلـه

"With peace," a formula for ending letters
ma` as-salaamah *(ma`as salaam ah)* مـع الـسـلامـة

"What Allah wishes" and it indicates a good omen, e.g. I get an A in a test, my mother would say:
mashaa Allaah *(maa shaa allaah)* مـا شـاء الـلـه

"May Allah bless Him and grant Him peace," used when mentioning Prophet Muhammed
sallal lahu `alayhi wa sallam
(sallal laaho `alayyhe wa sallam)
صـلـى الـلـه عـلـيـه وسـلـم

Literally meaning **"Old man"** – an honorific title widely used to denote scholars, as well as tribal chieftians and notables.
shaykh *(shaykh)* شـيـخ

When a person sneezes he/she says, **"alhamdulillaah (Praise be to Allah),"** a person who hears the sneeze says **"yarhamuka Allaah,"** a prayer for the sneezer which means **"May Allah have mercy on you."** The sneezer then replies **"yahdiina wa iyyaakum Allah"** which means **"May Allah give you and us the guidance."**
yarhamukal laah *(yar hamo kallaah)* يـرحـمـك الـلـه

PART 3

Words listing in alphabetical order

English	Romanized Arabic	Arabic
4 x 4 (engine)	rubaa`iyy	دفع رباعي
accident	h̲aadith	حادث
address	`unwaan	عنوان
after	ba`d	بعد
afternoon	ba`d az̲-z̲uhr	بعد الظهر
age	`umr	عمر
alcoholic	kuh̲uuliyy	كحولي
Alexandria	al-iskandariyyah	الإسكندرية
all	jamii`	جميع
Allow me	ismah̲ lii	اسمح لي
alone	wah̲iid	وحيد
a.m	s̲abaah̲an	صباحاً
ambassador	safiir	سفير
America	amriikaa	أمريكا
American	amriikiyy	أمريكي
anniversary	munaasabah /	مناسبة /
	dhikraa sanawiyyah	ذكرى سنوية
any	ayy	أي
apologize	a`tadhir	أعتذر
appointment	maw`id	موعد

English	Romanized Arabic	Arabic
April	Niisaan	نيسان
Arabian	\`arabiyy	عربي
Arabic	al-lughah al-\`arabiyyah	اللغة العربية
August	abb	آب
Australia	usturaalyaa	أستراليا
Australian	usturaaliyy	أسترالي
autumn	khariif	خريف
bag	haqiibah	حقيبة
bar	haanah	حانة
barber	hallaaq	حلاق
bathroom	hammaam	حمام
beautiful	jamiil / jamiilah	جميل / جميل
beer	ja\`\`ah / biirah	جعة / بيرة
before	qabl	قبل
begin	yabda’	يبدأ
behind	khalf	خلف
beside	bijaanib	بجانب
big	kabiir	كبير
bill	fatuurah	فاتورة
birthday	\`iid / yawm miilaad	عيد / يوم ميلاد
book *(n.)*	kitaab	كتاب
bookstore	maktabah	مكتبة
breakfast	iftaar	إفطار
bring, to	tuhdir	تحضر
Britain	briitaanyaa	بريطانيا

English	Romanized Arabic	Arabic
British	briitaaniyy	بريطاني
bus	haafilah	حافلة
business	`amal	عمل
businessman	rajul a`maal	رجل أعمال
buy, to	ashtarii	أشتري
by	`an	عن
Cairo	al-qaahirah	القاهرة
call (*n*)	ittisaal	اتصال
call, to	attasil	أتصل
Canada	kanadaa	كندا
Canadian	kanadiyy	كندي
car	sayyaarah	سيارة
card	bitaaqah	بطاقة
cash	naqdan	نقداً
check, to	uraaji`	أراجع
China	as-siin	الصين
Chinese	siiniyy	صيني
city	madiinah	مدينة
coffee	qahwah	قهوة
coffee shop	maqhaa	مقهى
cold (*adj.*)	baarid	بارد
come, to	ya'tii	يأتي
company	sharikah	شركة
computer	haasuub	حاسوب
cost (*n.*)	kulfah	كلفة
credit card	bitaaqat i'timaan	بطاقة ائتمان

English	Romanized Arabic	Arabic
Damascus	dimashq	دمشق
dawn	fajr	فجر
day after day	yawm ba`da yawm	يوم بعد يوم
day after tomorrow	ba`da ghad	بعد غد
daytime	nahaar	نهار
December	kaanuun awwal	كانون أول
dentist	tabiib asnaan	طبيب أسنان
dinner	`ashaa’	عشاء
doctor	tabiib	طبيب
drink, to	ashrab	أشرب
drinks	mashruubaat	مشروبات
driver	saa’iq	سائق
during	khilaal	خلال
Dutch	hulandiyy	هولندي
E-mail	bariid iliktruniyy	بريد إلكتروني
early	mubakkir	مبكر
Egypt	misr	مصر
eleventh	haadii `ashar	حادي عشر
embassy	safaarah	سفارة
enough	kaafii	كافي
evening	masaa’	مساء
every day	kulla yawm	كل يوم
excuse me	al-ma`dhirah	المعذرة
exhausted	murhaq	مرهق
expensive	ghaalii	غالي

English	Romanized Arabic	Arabic
family	\`aa'ilah	عــائــلــة
famous	mash-huur	مــشــهــور
far	ba\`iid	بــعــيــد
fare	ujrah	أجــرة
fast food	wajbah sari\`ah	وجــبــات ســريــعــة
father	abb	أب
father-in-law	hamuu	حــمو
Father's Day	\`iid al-abb	عــيــد الأب
favorite	mufaddal	مــفــضــل
fax	faaks	فــاكس
February	shubaat	شــبــاط
fifteenth	khaamis \`ashar	خــامــس عــشــر
fifth	khaamis	خــامــس
filling *(n.)*	hashwah	حــشــوة
first	awwal	أول
fourteenth	raabi\` \`ashar	رابــع عــشــر
fourth	raabi\`	رابــع
France	faransaa	فــرنــســا
French	faransiyy	فــرنــســي
Friday	al-jumu\`ah	الــجــمــعــة
from	min	مــن
front	amaam	أمــام
German	almaaniyy	ألــمــانــي
Germany	almaanyaa	ألــمــانــيــا
go, to	yadhhab	يــذهــب
going	dhahaab	ذهــاب

English	Romanized Arabic	Arabic
goodbye	ma` as-salaamah	مع السلامة
good evening	masaa' al-khayr	مساء الخير
good morning	sabaah al-khayr	صباح الخير
goodnight	tusbih `alaa khay	تصبح على خير
guidebooks	kutub irshadiyyah	كتب إرشادية
hair	sha`r	شعر
happy	sa`iid	سعيد
headache	sudaa`	صداع
hello	marhaban	مرحباً
help, to	yusaa`id	يساعد
here	hunaa	هنا
holiday	ijaazah	إجازة
home	bayt	بيت
hope, to	'aamal	آمل
hospital	mustashfaa	مستشفى
hot	haarr	حار
hotel	funduq	فندق
hour	saa`ah	ساعة
house	manzil	منزل
how	kayfa	كيف
how long	kam min al-waqt	كم من الوقت
how many	kam	كم
how much	kam	كم
humid	ratib	رطب
husband	zawj	زوج

English	Romanized Arabic	Arabic
iced	muthallaj	مثلج
I like	yu`jibunii	يعجبني
important	muhimm	مهم
international	duwaliyy	دولي
Internet	intirnit	إنترنت
introduction	ta`aaruf	تعارف
invitation	da`wah	دعوة
Islamic	islaamiyy	إسلامي
I would like	awaddu	أود
jacket	mi`taf	معطف
January	kaanuun thaanii	كانون ثاني
July	tamuuz	تموز
June	huzayraan	حزيران
know	a`rif	أعرف
language	lughah	لغة
late	muta'akh-khir	متأخر
leave, to	ughaadir	أغادر
little	qaliil	قليل
live, to	askun	أسكن
local	mahalliyy	محلي
look for, to	abhathu `an	أبحث
lost *(adj.)*	daa'i`	ضائع
loud	murtafi`	مرتفع
lunch	ghadaa'	غداء

English	Romanized Arabic	Arabic
Madam	sayyidah	سيدة
magazine	majallah	مجلة
man	rajul	رجل
manual	yadawiyy	يدوي
map	khariitah	خريطة
March	‘aadhaar	آذار
market	suuq	سوق
married *(adj.)*	mutazawwij	متزوج
maximum	uzmaa	عظمى
May	ayyaar	أيار
mean, to	a`nii	أعني
medicine	dawaa’	دواء
meet, to	altaqii	ألتقي
meeting	ijtimaa`	اجتماع
men’s toilet	hammaam rijaal	حمام رجال
mistake	khata’	خطأ
mobile phone	haatif naqqaal	هاتف نقال
moderate	mu`tadil	معتدل
moment	lahzah	لحظة
Monday	al-ithnayn	الإثنين
money	nuquud	نقود
monkey	qird	قرد
month	shahr	شهر
more	akthar	أكثر
morning	sabaah	صباح
mother	umm	أم
mother-in-law	hamaah	حماة

English	Romanized Arabic	Arabic
Mother's Day	`iid al-umm	عيد الأم
mouse	fa'rah	فأرة
mouth	famm	فم
move, to	ataharrak	أتحرك
movie	film	فيلم
museum	muthaf	متحف
music	musiiqaa	موسيقى
mustaches	shaarib	شارب
myself	nafsii	نفسي
name	ism	اسم
near	qariib	قريب
nearby	bil-qurb	بالقرب
nearest	aqrab	أقرب
need, to	ahtaaj	أحتاج
negotiable	qaabil lit-tafaawud	قابل للتفاوض
New Zealand	nyuuziilandah	نيوزيلندة
news	akhbaar	أخبار
newspaper	jariidah	جريدة
newsstand	kishk jaraa'id	كشك جرائد
nice	jamiil	جميل
night	layl	ليل
night club	naadii laylii	نادي ليلي
ninth	taasi`	تاسع
no	laa	لا
noon	zuhr	ظهر
north	shamaal	شمال

English	Romanized Arabic	Arabic
November	tishriin thaanii	تشرين ثاني
now	al’aan	الآن
number	`adad	عدد
nurse *(fem)*	mumarridah	ممرضة
occasion	munaasabah	مناسبة
October	tishriin awwal	تشرين أول
office	maktab	مكتب
old	kabiir bis-sin	كبير بالسن
one-way	ittijaah waahid	اتجاه واحد
open, to	yaftah	يفتح
opener	fattaahah	فتاحة
orange	burtuqaal	برتقال
order	talab	طلب
ordinal	tartiibiyy	ترتيبي
pair	zawj	زوج
parking	mawqif	موقف
passport	jawaaz safar	جواز سفر
paste *(n.)*	ma`juun	معجون
path	masaar	مسار
patient *(n.)*	mariid	مريض
pavement	rasiif	رصيف
pay, to	adfa`	أدفع
peace	salaam	سلام
pedestrians	mushaah	مشاة
pen	qalam	قلم

English	Romanized Arabic	Arabic
pharmacist	saydalaaniyy	صيدلاني
phone	haatif	هاتف
photograph	suurah	صورة
pills	hubuub	حبوب
pilot	tayyaar	طيار
place	makaan	مكان
please	rajaa'an	رجاءً
	law samaht	لو سمحت
	min fadlik	من فضلك
p.m.	masaa'an	مساءً
P.O Box	sunduuq bariid	صندوق بريد
police	shurtah	شرطة
policeman	shurtiyy	شرطي
post office	maktab bariid	مكتب بريد
postal address	`inwaan bariidiyy	عنوان بريدي
poster	mulsaq	ملصق
pound *(sterling)*	junayh	جنيه
prefer, to	ufaddil	أفضل
present *(n.)*	hadiyyah	هدية
presenter	muqaddim baraamij	مقدم برامج
president	ra'iis	رئيس
price	si`r	سعر
primary	ibtidaa'iyy	ابتدائي
printer	taabi`ah	طابعة
processor	mu`aalij	معالج
profession	mihnah	مهنة
program	barnaamij	برنامج

English	Romanized Arabic	Arabic
public toilet	hammaam `umuumiyy	حمام عمومي
pyramids	ahraamaat	أهرامات
quickly	bisur`ah	بسرعة
radio	midhyaa`	مذياع
railway	sikkah hadiidiyyah	سكة حديدية
rain *(n.)*	matar	مطر
raincoat	mi`taf matar	معطف مطر
rainy	maatir	ماطر
rate *(exchange)*	si’r sarf	سعر صرف
razor blades	shafraat	شفرات
reach, to	asil	أصل
read, to	aqra’	أقرأ
recommend, to	tuusii	توصي
receipt	wasl	وصل
reception	istiqbaal	استقبال
receptionist	muwazzaf istiqbaal	موظف استقبال
red	ahmar	أحمر
registered mail	bariid musta`jil	بريد مسجل
rent, to	asta’jir	أستأجر
representative	mumath-thil	ممثل
reservations	hujuuzaat	حجوزات
rest, to	artaah	أرتاح
restaurant	mat`am	مطعم

English	Romanized Arabic	Arabic
return *(n.)*	`awdah	عودة
rice	aruzz	أرز
right *(correct)*	yamiin	يمين
right	sahiih	صحيح
rinse *(n.)*	ghasuul	غسول
Riyadh	ar-riyaad	الرياض
road	tariiq	طريق
Roman	rumaaniyy	روماني
room	ghurfah	غرفة
run, to	arkud	أركض
salt	milh	ملح
satellite	qamar sinaa`iyy	قمر صناعي
Saturday	as-sabt	السبت
say, to	taquul	تقول
school	madrasah	مدرسة
screen	shaashah	شاشة
sea	bahr	بحر
seafood	ma'kuulaat bahriyyah	مأكولات بحرية
search *(n.)*	bahth	بحث
season	mawsim	موسم
seat	maq`ad	مقعد
seatbelt	hizaam amaan	حزام أمان
second	thaaniyah	ثانية
secondary	thaanawiyy	ثانوي
see, to	araa	أرى

English	Romanized Arabic	Arabic
send	ursil	أرسل
separate, to	yafsil	يفصل
September	ayluul	أيلول
series	musalsal	مسلسل
serious	khatiir	خطير
seventh	saabi`	سابع
shampoo	shaambu	شامبو
shave, to	ahliq	أحلق
shaving	hilaaqah	حلاقة
shirt	qamiis	قميص
shoes	ahdhiyah	أحذية
shop *(n.)*	dukkaan	دكان
shopping	tasawwuq	تسوق
should	yanbaghii	ينبغي
show *(n.)*	barnaamij idhaa`iyy/ tilfizyuniyy	برنامج إذاعي / تلفزيوني
sick	mariid	مريض
Sir	sayyid	سيد
sister	ukht	أخت
sit down, to	ijlis	اجلس
sixth	saadis	سادس
sleep, to	anaam	أنام
slowly	bi but'	ببطء
snake	af`aa	أفعى
snow *(n.)*	thalj	ثلج
soda	sudaa	صودا
soft drink	mashruub ghaaziyy	مشروب غازي

English	Romanized Arabic	Arabic
soft music	musiiqaa haadi'ah	موسيقى هادئة
someone	shakhsun maa / ahaduhum	شخص ما / أحدهم
something	shay'	شيء
son	ibn	ابن
sorry	'aasif	آسف
soup	saabuun	صابون
south	januub	جنوب
souvenir	tadhkaar	تذكار
speak, to	atahaddath	أتحدث
spring	rabii`	ربيع
stairs	daraj	درج
stamp	taabi`	طابع
start	yabda'	يبدأ
station	mahattah	محطة
stay, to	abqaa	أبقى
steam	bukhaar	بخار
steering wheel	miqwad	مقود
step *(n.)*	khutwah	خطوة
stolen, has/ have	saraqa	سرق
stomachache	maghs	مغص
stop, to	qiff	قف
storm	`aasifah	عاصفة
stroll, to	uharwil	أهرول
student	taalib	طالب
study, to	adrus	أدرس

English	Romanized Arabic	Arabic
sugar	sukkar	سـكـر
suite	janaah	جـنـاح
summer	sayf	صـيـف
Sunday	al-ahad	الأحـد
sure	muta'akkid	مـتـأكـد
swimming pool	birkat sibaahah	بـركـة سـبـاحـة
syrup	sharaab	شـراب
system	nizaam	نـظـام
table	taawilah	طـاولـة
take, to	'aakhudh	آخـذ
taxi	sayyaarat ujrah	سـيـارة أجـرة
tea	shaay	شـاي
teeth	asnaan	أسـنـان
tell, to	yaquul	يـقـول
temperature	darajat haraarah	درجـة حـرارة
tenth	`aashir	عـاشـر
terminal	qaa`at intizaar	قـاعـة انتظار
thanks	shukran	شـكـراً
there	hunaak	هـنـاك
third	thaalith	ثـالـث
thirsty	`atshaan	عـطـشـان
thirteenth	thaalith `ashar	ثـالـث عـشـر
this	haadhaa / haadhihi	هـذا / هـذه
Thursday	al-khamiis	الـخـمـيـس
ticket	tadhkarah	تـذكـرة

English	Romanized Arabic	Arabic
ticket officer	muwaz-zaf at-tadhaakir	موظف التذاكر
tiger	namir	نمر
time	waqt	وقت
timetable	jadwal zamaniyy	جدول زمني
tire *(n.)*	itaar	إطار
tired *(adj.)*	mut`ab	متعب
toasted	muhammas	محمص
today	al-yawm	اليوم
toilet	hammaam	حمام
tomorrow	ghadan	غداً
tooth	sinn	سن
toothache	alam asnaan	ألم أسنان
tour	jawlah	جولة
tour guide	daliil siyaahiyy	دليل سياحي
tourist	saa'ih	سائح
toys	al`aab	ألعاب
traffic	muruur	مرور
traffic light	ishaarah daw'iyyah	إشارة ضوئية
train *(n.)*	qitaar	قطار
travel	usaafir	أسافر
travelers' check	shiik siyaahiyy	شيك سياحي
trip	rihlah	رحلة
Tuesday	ath-thulaathaa'	الثلاثاء
TV	tilfaaz	تلفاز
twelfth	thaanii `ashar	ثاني عشر

English	Romanized Arabic	Arabic
umbrella	mizallah	مظلة
uncle *(father's side)*	`amm	عم
uncle *(mother's side)*	khaal	خال
under	taht	تحت
understand	afham	أفهم
university	jaami`ah	جامعة
urgent	taari'	طارئ
use, to	astakhdim	أستخدم
vacant	shaaghir	شاغر
Valentine day	`iid al-hubb	عيد الحب
vegetable	khudaar	خضار
very	jiddan	جداً
view	tutill	تطل
voice	sawt	صوت
wait, to	antazir	أنتظر
waiter	naadil	نادل
waitress	naadilah	نادلة
walk, to	amshii	أمشي
want, to	uriid	أريد
watch, to	ushaahid	أشاهد
watch *(n.)*	saa`ah	ساعة
water	maa'	ماء
wave	mawjah	موجة
way	tariiq	طريق
we	nahnu	نحن

English	Romanized Arabic	Arabic
weather	jaww	جو
weather forecast	nashrah jawwiyyah	نشرة جوية
website	mawqi` iliktruniyy	موقع إلكتروني
wedding	zawaaj	زواج
Wednesday	al-arbi`aa’	الأربعاء
week	usbuu`	أسبوع
weekend	`utlat nihaayat al-usbuu`	عطلة نهاية الأسبوع
welcome	ahlan wa sahlan	أهلا وسهلا
well	hasanan	حسناً
west	gharb	غرب
western	gharbiyy	غربي
what	maa / maadhaa	ما / ماذا
wheel	`ajal	عجل
when	mataa	متى
where	ayna	أين
which	ayyu	أي
whisky	wiskii	ويسكي
white	abyad	أبيض
who	man	من
wife	zawjah	زوجة
wind	riyaah	رياح
window	naafidhah	نافذة
wine	nabiidh	نبيذ
winter	shitaa’	شتاء

English	Romanized Arabic	Arabic
without	biduun	بــدون
women's toilet	hammaam sayyidaat	حـمـام سـيـدات
work, to	a'mal	أعـمـل
write, to	aktub	أكـتـب
year	sanah	سـنـة
yes	na`am	نـعـم
yesterday	ams	أمـس
you *(dual)*	antumaa	أنـتـمـا
you *(pl. fem.)*	antunna	أنـتـن
you *(pl. masc.)*	antum	أنـتـم
you *(sing. fem.)*	anti	أنـتِ
you *(sing. masc.)*	anta	أنـتَ
zebra	himaar wahshiyy	حـمـار وحـشـي
zoo	hadiiqat hayawaanaat	حـديـقـة حـيـوانـات